E. W. Bu

D1045635

Eden Revival

DAVID M. BECKMANN

Foreword by William J. Danker

Eden Revival

Spiritual Churches
in Ghana

Publishing House
St. Louis   London

Concordia Publishing House, St. Louis, Missouri
Concordia Publishing House Ltd., London, E. C. 1
Copyright © 1975 Concordia Publishing House

MANUFACTURED IN THE UNITED STATES OF AMERICA

Library of Congress Cataloging in Publication Data

Beckmann, David M
    Eden Revival.

    Bibliography: p.
    1. Independent churches – Ghana. 2. Eden Revival
Church. I. Title.
BR1463.G5B42   266'.009667   73-83085
ISBN 0-570-03197-4

Contents

Foreword

EDEN REVIVAL is not only a detailed case study of a particularly intriguing spiritual church, but a concise handbook on the Christian movement in Ghanaian society.

Students of religion, history, culture, psychology, and anthropology, as well as those who seek for the African origins of black soul and religion in the New World, will find this an important study. It will also attract those interested in Africa, in missions, and the church in west Africa.

David Beckmann is well schooled and well traveled. At Yale University he won a top overseas fellowship. Drawn to Africa, he focused on the independent churches, spending months as a member of the household of Brother Yeboa, charismatic head of Eden Revival Church.

Returning from his fieldwork in Ghana, he expanded his research to include Pentecostalism in general, and later traveled to the West Indies to compare indigenous churches there with those he observed in Ghana.

Readers of EDEN REVIVAL are privileged to share in the first major work of a promising author.

WILLIAM J. DANKER, *Director*
Center for World Christian Interaction

Preface

African independent churches invite the attention of anyone interested in contemporary African culture or politics, Christian mission, Pentecostalism, or Afro-American studies. Independent churches may be the most dynamic element in African religion, apparently growing faster than Protestant and Catholic churches in many parts of the continent. Millions of Africans are now involved in 5,000 or 6,000 independent churches.[1] It is impossible to understand contemporary African culture without knowing about independent churches.

These churches are an intriguing cultural parallel to political and economic nationalism. The first independent churches were started by some of the best educated, most progressive Africans of the 19th century. Later independent churchmen, along with political nationalists, have reasserted traditional African culture, while at the same time modernizing by organizing across tribal lines, countering irrational beliefs, successfully integrating African and European culture, and establishing new schools and businesses. Independent churches have gained strength along with the rise of nationalist sentiment, and their popularity has increased markedly since the achievement of political independence in the 1960's.

African indigenous churches may be of considerable importance to the future of Christianity. Almost half the people of sub-Saharan Africa are Christian, and at a time when Christianity seems barely to be holding its own in Europe and North America, it has become Africa's fastest-growing religion. If present trends continue, most of the Christians in the world at the turn of the century will not be white. The numerical and creative center of Christianity is shifting to the Third World, notably

Africa.[2] While Bishop Stephen Neill is, no doubt, right in contending that the chief ingathering of new Christians is by the main-line churches, independent African churches will be an influential element in future African Christianity.

Africa has already influenced Christianity powerfully through Pentecostalism. Pentecostalism is in part derived from Africa through the influence of black people in the United States. Trance found a place of unprecedented prominence within Christian worship during the Second Great Awakening in the United States; its introduction into Christianity was associated with the first major successes in evangelism among black slaves. Trance is prevalent in traditional African religion, and some slaves continued to value it after their conversion. Pentecostalism, distinguished primarily by "speaking in tongues," a type of trance modeled after several passages in the New Testament, began early in the 20th century in a revival led by black people. Since then the Pentecostal movement has shown awesome missionary strength, especially in those areas most influenced by African culture. There are 25 countries where more than one precent of the population is Pentecostal, and 22 of them are African or include considerable numbers of Afro-Americans.[3] In general, Pentecostal missionaries introduced Biblical arguments for trance in Christian worship to indigenous churches as well as to their own mission churches. In Ghana, for example, indigenous churches had included fasting, visions, and other African elements in their piety, but trance was first justified by missionaries from the Apostolic Church. Now virtually all the indigenous churches of Ghana are Pentecostal, and familiarity with them is essential to a complete understanding of the world Pentecostal movement. Their worship is graced not only by "tongues" and healing, but also by more totally involving forms of trance, as well as dancing, dreams, visions, divination, and the curing of witches.

Independent churches in Africa are a crucial element in Afro-American studies too. Most Afro-Americans in the West Indies and the United States are affiliated with all-black churches which are often strikingly similar to Africa's indigenous churches.

10

Communication between Africans and Afro-Americans has been severely limited since the end of the slave trade, yet Africans and Afro-Americans have everywhere withdrawn from white churches to worship in their own distinctive way. A Ghanaian man who is used to spiritual churches at home would feel fairly comfortable at a storefront service in Harlem. A lady from South Africa with a health problem would not have too much difficulty finding a healer in Trinidad somewhat like the Christian "prophets" in her own country. The unity of Afro-Christianity throughout Africa, the West Indies, and the United States is not generally recognized, but in fact it constitutes one of the most extensive and influential religious traditions in the world.

This book focuses on independent African churches in Ghana. The movement has burgeoned in Ghana during the last years. The very first independent church in all of Africa was started in Ghana in 1862. The movement was not prominent, however, until about 1957, when Ghana won her national independence. A few independent churches were formed in Ghana in the middle 1950's; seven African-led churches were reported in Accra just before national independence.[4] By 1970 there were at least 100 such churches in Accra, and about 200 others scattered throughout the country. Probably 300,000 or 400,000 Ghanaians have firmly committed themselves to independent churches, and at least twice as many again have in some way been influenced by the movement. I decided to make a fresh report on this part of the African independent church movement, since the fieldwork for the previous major study of indigenous churches in Ghana (C. G. Baeta's *Prophetism in Ghana*) was done in 1958, when the movement was only beginning.

Are these new churches in Ghana similar to Afro-Christian churches elsewhere? Are they rightfully considered part of the Pentecostal movement? What contributions might they make to world Christianity? Is their religious independence connected with political nationalism? How are they related to Ghana's religious heritage? These are the questions this study set out to answer.

The first section of the book is a macroanalysis of the development of the independent church movement in Ghana. The second section is a microanalysis of Eden Revival Church, one of the most prominent of the many African churches that have appeared since Ghana's independence. The first section, a historical overview, provides background material and a preliminary understanding; the second section, a case study, focuses on one church and gives fuller, more detailed information. My fieldwork (1969–70) involved visits to comparable religious bodies in Asia and east Africa, several months of traveling in Ghana, and four months as a guest in the Accra home of the founder and leader of Eden Revival Church.

There are several key terms used in this book that need definition at the outset. The terms "African independent church" and "indigenous church" are often used in the literature on the subject to refer to an African religious group that has broken away from the foreign missions and mission-related churches. These terms are slightly confusing, however, because most of the churches in historical continuity with European missions are now financially independent, while many of the schismatic, so-called "independent churches" have sought and are receiving aid from abroad.

The terms "independent church" and "indigenous church" are seldom used in Ghana except by people who have read about such churches in other parts of Africa. Most people in Ghana, including the leaders of the movement, do not know about similar churches in other parts of the continent. In common parlance the indigenous churches together with similar Pentecostal churches imported from Nigeria and the United States are called "spiritual churches."

The expression "spiritual church" (in Twi, *sunsum Asɔre*) is a poor translation of a west African concept. The *sunsum* refers to that part of the human personality which wanders away from the body in dreams and visions. A strong *sunsum* is said to be the best defense against malicious spiritual powers. The Holy Spirit is known as *sunsum kronkron;* glossolalia, ecstasy, visions, spiritual protection, and miraculous healing are thought to be His main province.[5] Those churches which concern themselves extensively with such things, most of them indigenous and comparatively new, are called "spiritual churches." On the other hand, the churches which do not practice spiritualism, notably the Methodists, Presbyterians, and Roman Catholics in Ghana, are usually called "orthodox churches."

I am indebted to Charles Yeboa-Korie, who welcomed me into his home, shared his meals, and generously passed many hours with me, opening himself and his church to examination more intimate than most. Scores of members of Eden Revival Church shared their time, their knowledge, and their affection. Particularly helpful were Victor and Amelia Gyimah, H. O. Beeko, Mary Asante, Susan Ofori-Ata, and Joshua Williams. I feel closest to J. R. Anquandah, secretary of Eden and director of Eden's schools, with whom I could always talk freely.

The John Courtney Murray Fellowship Committee of Yale University made the year financially possible. While I was in Ghana I was enrolled at the University of Ghana, Institute of African Studies, with K. A. Opoku as my adviser.

The Lutheran mission staff in Ghana, especially Walter Schmidt, James Dretke, Walter DeMoss, and their wives were kind and helpful. Edwin and Irene Weaver were always a source of information and encouragement.

I am most deeply indebted to William J. Danker. He has been an invaluable teacher, friend, and advocate in the process of research, writing, and publication. Grants from the World Mission Institute, of which he was director, subsidized my research in the West Indies and the publication of this volume. His student assistant, Lee Griess, researched several corrections.

My warm thanks to Bishop Stephen Neill of the Anglican Church, Al Krass of the United Church of Christ, former missionary to Ghana, and Walter Schmidt of The Lutheran Church—Missouri Synod, who read this work in whole or part before it went to press. They helped to improve it, but should not be taxed for its shortcomings.

My new wife Janet patiently allowed me time to work on revisions, but never left me alone so long that the task became tedious.

PART I

The Spiritual Church Movement

CHAPTER ONE

Antecedents of the Spiritual Churches

Spiritual churches are best understood in the context of African religion and its intriguing evolution during the past century. This chapter outlines traditional Ghanaian religion, the genuinely sacrificial efforts of early missionaries, the fantastic successes of later African prophets, the connections between Christian mission and colonialism, and the revival of paganism in the 1940's. Each major stage of Ghana's religious development — traditional religion, Christian mission, and the medicine shrines — has had its own direct effect on contemporary spiritual churches.

Precolonial Religion

Christians everywhere tend to bring the best of their cultures into their churches, and Ghana's spiritual church leaders are usually proud that their services are shaped by African religiosity and graced by African music and dance. They virulently oppose most aspects of traditional African religion, however, and sometimes resent suggestions that they have inherited much from it. Since spiritual church Christians may be somewhat less prone to resort to shrines and charms in emergencies than Ghanaians who attend orthodox churches, spiritual church leaders can argue convincingly that they are moving away from traditional religion and toward the Bible. Yet they approach the Bible with some of the needs which traditional religion satisfied for their parents or grandparents, and they find in the Bible cultures that are not altogether different from those traditional in Ghana. A Ghanaian easily relates to the beliefs about the supernatural, the agricultural imagery, the fierce tribalism, and strong family ties he finds in the Bible. The incarnation of the Christian message which is resulting from a fresh reading of the Bible by spiritual churchmen is more radically continuous with Ghana's past than any self-conscious program of Africanization could be.

The anthropological studies done in the 1920's while the British were consolidating their rule give us a fairly clear idea what the religious life of the tribes of southern Ghana was like before colonialism and Christianity made their impact.[1] It was anything but static:

> Anyone who has attempted to compile a history of even one small town anywhere in Ghana knows that few towns and states did not begin as heterogeneous settlements of refugees, displaced persons, prisoners of war, slaves, traders, remnants of defeated armies and so on, some of them immigrants from great distance, and all of them bringing fragments of widely divergent religions. West Africa has always been in a state of flux; none of the communities has ever been so stably settled that it could not accept and assess with equanimity another new fragment of religion.[2]

Ghanaian religion was then—as it is now—decentralized, polytheistic, and diverse. Certain preoccupations and ideas circulated among all the peoples now involved in the spiritual church movement. Therefore we can discuss a common religious heritage.

In general, the concerns of African religion are this-worldly, primarily health and fertility. West African religion throbs with an almost fierce vitality. The libation prayer of an Ashanti king at an annual festival recorded by Rattray is representative of the sort of petitions Ghanaians are used to addressing to the spirits:

16

Friday, Stool of Kings, I sprinkle water upon you, may your
   power return sharp and fierce. Grant that when I and
   another meet in battle it be as when I met Denkyira; you let
   me cut off his head.
The edges of the years have met,
   I pray for life.
May the nation prosper.
May the women bear children.
May the hunters kill meat.
We who dig for gold, let us get gold to dig, and grant that I get
   some for the upkeep of my kingship.[3]

There was no self-abnegation in the king's prayer. He called for
power, life, prosperity, fertility, success, and wealth. The vitality
of west African religion may have been one reason why Afro-
American slaves were able to survive capture, brutal transport
to the Americas, slavery — and still keep dancing.

God (in Twi *Onyame*) was thought to be the father of all
things and source of all life, but people who follow the old ways
seldom approach *Onyame* ritually. Instead, petitions are addressed to his many "sons" and to ancestor spirits. The "sons"
of God, or small gods *(abosom)*, vary greatly in personality and
power. Many are spirits of particular places, rivers, or families,
but the cults of powerful gods spread far beyond their points of
origin. The ancestors, especially royal spirits, are regularly
offered libations and petitioned for the continued fertility of the
family and village.

Charms and amulets *(suman)* rank below the spirits in theory,
but charms were probably always the first resort of most people.
The border between the weakest gods and most powerful magic
is blurred, but in general charms are thought to be impersonal,
less powerful than deities, less demanding morally and ritually.

Most traditional religious activity is ad hoc and private. When
asking about a particular deity I was often told that a priest or
elder in the house "takes care of it." Religious specialists dutifully
sacrifice to small gods, and priests are regularly possessed, but
most people do not bother about such things until they are in
need. Then they seek out a trusted specialist for advice and

a ritual prescription. Individuals satisfy private religious needs individually.

Group religious activities, on the other hand, center around common concerns and tend to be pure celebrations. Outdoorings (initiation of babies) and funerals seem to be the festivals least impaired by the changes of the last 50 years. Funerals are still probably the major social events in Ghana and people in Accra frequently return to their villages to mourn with their relatives. Each village also has its own ritual cycle. The local small gods may demand days of observation, and at least once a year everyone turns out for a magnificent celebration in honor of the royal ancestors. Over half the workers in Ghana are migrants,[4] however, and this tremendous mobility has crippled the old town and village celebrations. Akans and Ewes in Accra may know little about the customs observed in their home towns.

Christianity

Early Mission Enclaves

Many Ghanaians still believe and practice traditional religion, but the old ways have been under the seige of Christian missions for over a century. The first mission enclaves were established in Ghana in the 1830's and 1840's. The earliest missionaries met with little numerical success, but they made a lasting mark on Christianity in Ghana. The African independent church movement is rooted in the spirit of the early missionaries.

Africa was dangerous to white men then. The continent was mysterious to Europeans, and tropical diseases killed one missionary after another. The fact that missionaries kept coming, in spite of almost certain death, points up the extraordinary and genuine zeal of the mission pioneers.

Their remarkable fervor was a product of the 19th-century evangelical revivals in Europe. These revivals were characterized by personal religious experience and individual interpretation of the Bible, rather than official ritual and dogma. Until the very late 19th century nearly all the missionaries were evangelicals: Methodists, "low church" Anglicans, German and Swiss pietists. The tone of their faith, startlingly similar to that of contemporary spiritual churches, rings clear in the words the first Methodist missionary to Ghana wrote in his diary on the day of his arrival in 1834:

> I want more of God, more of his life in my soul. I see its necessity more than ever, a burning charity for all mankind . . . Who can convert these? The power of God; that is everything I want; all other things are absorbed in this consideration.[5]

During the first half of the 19th century evangelical missionaries set up a handful of mission stations in south and west Africa, including the Basel and Methodist stations in Ghana. In Ghana they started little schools, built roads, and introduced agricultural techniques (including a new crop, cocoa). They recorded local customs and worked in local languages. The New Testament was translated into all the major languages of south Ghana by 1900; Ga was the fifth, Twi the seventh African language, into which the entire Bible was translated.[6]

It was undoubtedly the intention of the early missionaries that the African churches would quickly become independent. White men simply could not live in Africa then, so training Africans to lead the mission churches was a matter of life and death.[7]

Also, the missionaries and the evangelical movement which supplied them were theologically committed to personal responsibility, rather than church authority, in religion. The evangelical revivals were primarily movements of the lower and middle classes of Europe. The missionaries themselves were almost all artisans or mechanics, often hastily trained at second-rate seminaries. The evangelical revivals were, in part, rebellions against the gentry's religious domination. The upper classes tended to scorn the emotionalism of evangelical worship and the ignorance of revival preachers.[8] Some of the evangelicals, notably the Methodists, founded churches to suit their own economic class just as Africans were later to form independent churches for themselves. The evangelicals who remained in the established churches were continually fending off aristocratic critics and quarreling with church officials.[9]

The missionaries moved quickly to replace themselves with African clergy. Nevertheless, even then there were occasional schisms. Already in 1819 Nova Scotian Negro settlers in Sierra Leone withdrew from the Wesleyan Missionary Society over the issue of white missionary arrogance.[10] In 1862 the first known secession of native Africans occurred in what is now Ghana; a few converts withdrew from the mission for a short while. They objected to lax discipline with regard to drinking and to the dues they were expected to pay the mission. They called themselves the Methodist Society and were known as "Water Drinkers." [11]

Imperial Christianity and African Churches

African independent churches became significant in the years after 1885, when European governments were gobbling up African territory. European medicine had by then developed defenses against tropical diseases, and white men had a reasonable chance of survival in Africa. Wealthy, well-educated young men flocked to Africa as both colonial officials and missionaries.[12] The new aristocratic missionaries shared the imperialistic attitudes of their fellows in the colonial governments and generally believed the racist ideas that were then considered scientific.

These new missionaries were ill-disposed toward any kind of African independence, and their arrival in force met with a flurry of schisms between 1890 and 1920. Many educated second- and third-generation African Christians resented the increased missionary paternalism and formed their own churches.[13] These independent churches were called "African churches" in west Africa, "Ethiopian churches" in south Africa (all of Africa being identified with Ethiopia, since it is the African nation most frequently mentioned in the Bible). The movement received aid and encouragement from Afro-Americans who already had developed mature black independent churches.

This first stage of the independent church movement dates from 1895 to 1910 with similar schisms occurring occasionally until the end of colonial rule. It was characterized by African-led churches that remained European in doctrine and liturgy. Many

20

of them, especially those keen on converting fellow Africans from traditional religion, allowed polygamy. But the secessionists did not, in general, reject European culture; rather they wanted to be more like Europeans than they could be in a paternalistic situation. Most of the secessionists had grown up under the tutelage of the early evangelical missionaries, and they were simply putting the original mission plans into action.

Most of the first independent churches began either in Lagos, Nigeria, or Johannesburg, South Africa. In Sierra Leone the churches had already been transferred to African control before the 1890's. Elsewhere the missions were too young and the class of educated Africans too small to counter the change in mission policy with large-scale secessions.

In Ghana only three small African churches were formed: the National Baptist Church, founded by Mark Christian Hayford in 1898; the African Methodist Episcopal Zion Church, brought to Ghana by a West Indian in the same year; and the Nigrition Church, founded in 1907 by J. B. Anaman. All of these churches espoused the ideology developed during similar schisms in Nigeria and South Africa. It was clearly expressed by one of the early independent African ministers in Ghana:

> Our church is indeed an entirely Negro Church, organized by Negroes for Negroes, manned, governed, controlled, and supported by Negro energy, intellect, liberality and contribution. In fact, it is the sentiment of the church, that however great may be the friendship of any white man, in the well-being, christianization, and enlightenment of the Negro race . . . he cannot successfully reach the emotional feelings of the mass of our people.[14]

The issue which sparked the Nigrition secession was singing bands. Today nearly every Protestant congregation in Ghana has a choir which follows the style of indigenous folk-singing, but it once seemed improper to the missionaries. J. B. Anaman convinced a congregation, already angry because the missionaries would not allow their singing band to perform in church, to become independent with "singing and a form of worship that would appeal to the idiosyncrasies and customs, laws, and privileges of the native."

Except for singing bands, however, the first African independent churches in Ghana were just like the missions in doctrine and liturgy. Since the missionaries in Ghana were less paternalistic than white people in the United States and South Africa, virulent antiwhite sentiment was never expressed by independent churchmen in Ghana.[15] There were always amicable social relations and even pulpit exchanges between the missions and independent churches. All three original independent churches were tiny, and only the African Methodist Episcopal Zion (AMEZ), which receives aid from American blacks, survived.

Personal ambitions were a factor in the establishment of all three churches. For example, the early nationalist J. K. Aggrey, sent to the United States for training to be the first AMEZ minister, decided to stay and continue studies there rather than return to his post. Mark Hayford traveled to England, France, and the United States seeking funds for his National Baptist Church, always getting enough to continue his travels, but seldom sending any funds back to his feeble church and school in Ghana. To recognize self-interested motives of these leaders does not, however, minimize their accomplishment: proof that African Christians could manage their own church affairs.

Mission Growth and Prophetism

The efforts of the early evangelical missionaries may have been noble, but those of their successors were much more effective. Christianity made its major gains only after English businessmen and colonial officers dominated Ghana. Ghanaians had traded with Europeans for centuries, but due to the military might of Ashanti and the reluctance of the British to become unnecessarily involved in the interior, parts of Ghana remained independent into the 20th century. The British were mostly interested in coastal trade, so even the final conquest of Ashanti brought relatively few major changes to the interior.

The Akans were finally caught up in the international market when they began exporting cocoa. The following figures, cocoa production in five-year averages by tons for the years 1891 – 1934, show the explosion of cocoa production: [16]

Years	Tons
1891 – 1895	5
1896 – 1900	230
1901 – 1905	3,172
1906 – 1910	14,784
1911 – 1915	51,819
1916 – 1920	106,072
1921 – 1925	186,329
1926 – 1930	218,895
1931 – 1934	336,088

Inspired by this new productivity, the colonial government under Sir Gordon Guggisberg, governor, in the 1920's, made "development" its policy. The transportation network was dramatically extended, the volume of trade raised, and African participation in the colonial regime increased.

In many parts of Africa Islam replaced traditional religion as people became involved in the process of modernization, but not in Ghana. Only 12 percent of the population is Moslem.[17] Most Ghanaian Moslems are northerners who have migrated to Ghana's cities. Having left their home deities, they are inclined to a universal religon. The southern tribes, which are predominately Christian, are also wealthier than the northern tribes. Northerners, often snubbed or ill-treated by Ghanaian Christians, tend to join mosques rather than churches.[18]

Some colonial governors preferred that Africans become Moslem rather than Christian and encouraged Islam by dealing through Moslem middlemen; Islam prospered in northern Nigeria and Tanzania partly for this reason. Ghana's colonial governors, however, subsidized mission schools and established secular schools. Education was *the* way to a job in the government or in commercial companies and the entrance pass into the emergent native ruling class. Since many schools were mission supervised, students often became Christian.

Even today membership in the Presbyterian Church of Ghana, which has been most heavily involved in school administration, is three-fourths children, although half the population is under 16.[19] The imbalance is due to the exodus of students upon graduation. Even though Christianity has remained for many classroom converts as superficial as their school uniforms, something to be donned for show and taken off at home, education and Christianity are inseparable in the minds of most Ghanaians. To learn to read still means primarily to read the Bible, and to have gone to school (with the status that implies) also means to be a Christian.

The growth of the churches closely followed the demand for schools. But hospitals, the other mission offering almost universally desired in Africa, were not significant in the growth of Ghanaian Christianity. In the entire nation there was only one mission hospital before World War II.[20] Since then, mostly after independence, the government and the churches have greatly expanded modern medical facilities, but even in 1964 there were only about 100 hospitals in all of Ghana (a third of them church-related) and only one doctor for every 12,000 people.[21] Faith healing in the spiritual churches today may fill a gap in Christian life; the missionaries, by and large, condemned traditional medicine without providing an alternative.

Statistics for the Methodist Church, the only readily available mission figures for these early years of colonial development and church growth, show that more than seven times as many Africans converted to Methodist Christianity in the 30 years 1910–40 than had converted in the previous 75 years of work in Ghana.[22] All the missions experienced mass conversions after about 1910, and all of them were grossly understaffed. Hastily trained evangelists and catechists had to be trusted to teach the thousands who suddenly wanted to be baptized and send their children to school. The leadership of the movement into Christianity was indigenous by default.

Charismatic religious leaders, similar to Old Testament prophets in style, were probably familiar figures in Africa before Christianity arrived. Itinerant preachers, some Christian and some pagan, can still be seen — usually in colorful costumes — on the streets and roads of Ghana. During the mass movement toward Christianity that accompanied the consolidation of colonial rule in 1910 – 30, for the first time some of these African prophets began to preach Christian doctrines. They often taught without any supervision from European missionaries, and probably met with more numerical success.

Several powerful Christian-influenced prophets appeared in South Africa, notably Isaiah Shembe, who was hailed as messiah by thousands of followers. Smaller sects clustered around hundreds of less powerful leaders; today there are over 1,500 "Zionist" churches in South Africa, characterized by charismatic leadership, emotional and ecstatic worship, and a liberal borrowing from Bantu religion. Similar churches were first reported in Kenya during that period also.

Christianity arrived in central Africa at about the same time as imperial politics and exploitative companies. Religious movements set off by the social dislocation were therefore less affected by orthodox Christianity than those where missionaries had done prior work. African prophets and witch-hunters suddenly appeared in strength in various parts of Zambia, Zaire, and the People's Republic of Congo, often preaching a few newly learned Christian notions and very occasionally inspiring incidents of antiwhite violence. Droves of people rushed to hear Simon Kimbangu in eastern Zaire, and long after he was imprisoned they listened to a series of similar, but often less orthodox, prophets.[23]

William Wade Harris, one of the most influential preachers in history, began work in West Africa at this crucial time. He was a Grebo from Liberia, called to preach the Gospel while in prison for protesting the government's policy toward his tribe. He had little success in his own country; but when he traveled across Ivory Coast in 1914, people in village after village burned their fetishes and were baptized.

He wore a long robe and carried a bamboo cross. He had the power to heal and cast out demons, but he was primarily a preacher. His message was simple: destroy fetishes and be baptized. The French government feared the subversive potential of Harris' mass movement, so they deported him and systematically burned the churches of his converts. Nevertheless, Methodist missionaries arriving 20 years later discovered 50,000 of his followers still worshiping regularly.[24]

Harris spent several months of 1914 in southwest Ghana. He directed his converts to join the missions. Some of them became Roman Catholics. The Methodist missionaries in Ghana were exceptionally open-minded about African prophets, and many of Harris' converts, thousands of people, became Methodists.[25] Others, particularly polygamists, disregarded Harris' directions to join the missions and formed the first spiritual churches in Ghana, called *Nkansa*. There is little record of what these *Nkansa* churches were like originally, but in many villages along the road from Takoradi to Axim large distinctive white crosses still signal the presence of *Nkansa* congregations. In 1958 Baeta studied one loosely organized group of them, The Twelve Apostles' Church. He concluded that the *Nkansa* were by then very much like pagan shrines, except for the symbolic use of the Bible.[26]

It should be noted that Ivory Coast, one of the areas of west Africa least exposed to Europe through trade and missions, was ruthlessly conquered in 1910–14. To pacify the area, whole villages were resettled and recalcitrant chiefs deported. Almost immediately the French began drafting thousands of Ivoirians for World War I, so many that the colonial governor himself called the effort a "manhunt." [27]

Southwest Ghana, too, was in upheaval when Harris passed through. The economy of the region had been revolutionized only about 15 years before by the timber industry. In 1887 timber was exported from the area for the first time:

> Exports increased so dramatically that by 1894 they had reached the astonishing volume of about 45,000 cubic feet. The timber industry was fully established. Numerous timber concessions were taken by foreign capitalists, labour was readily attracted from both inside and outside the country. . . . After the 1890's the volume of exports depended primarily

on the state of demand in the consuming countries of Western Europe and the United States of America. Thus exports, after reaching the remarkably high level of about 3 million cubic feet in 1913, dropped to less than half that volume during the First World War.[28]

The collapse of the timber market in 1915 is shown clearly in the figure below: [29]

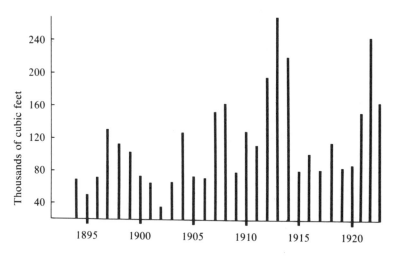

TIMBER PRODUCTION 1894—1923

Given the west African search for this-worldly well-being in religion and a proclivity to discard discredited deities in favor of perhaps more powerful imported gods, the economic crisis could very well have predisposed Harris' listeners to conversion.

The other famous early African prophet in Ghana, Samson Opong, accompanied the superintendent of the Methodist mission throughout central Ghana. He converted 10,000 people in two years. The Methodist yearbook of 1921 reported:

> From Ashanti comes the news of a great spiritual awakening. It began with the arrival of a remarkable man, a native of Northwest Ashanti, by name Samson Opon. He is manifestly a prophet

whom "God hath raised from among his brethren." Thousands have flocked to hear him, and through his message have been led to Christ. At the time these notes were written, more than ten thousand of all ages have given in their names desiring Christian instruction. All Ashanti is stirred, and in villages far beyond the range of the preacher's itinerary the Divine Spirit is working, and every day brings its own contingent of enquiries from afar. In many places whole villages have renounced and surrendered their idols and fetishes, and these are publicly burnt. Stories reach us of whole communities assembling themselves together on Sundays, waiting, waiting, waiting for someone to come along who will tell them the meaning of the new aspirations and strange desires which possess their hearts, and at last, as darkness falls, go their several ways hungry and unfed.[30]

The circumstances surrounding Opong in Ashanti (central Ghana) were similar to those in southwest Ghana, where Harris preached five years earlier. The Ashanti economy was also being transformed, in this case by the export of cocoa. The international market for most raw materials is unstable, and this is especially true for cocoa. The cocoa boom was in full swing, but the price dropped sharply for the first time in 1920. The same Methodist annual which described villages waiting for someone "to tell them the meaning of the new aspirations and strange desires which possess their hearts" also mentioned that it had been an "unprecedented year of trade depression."

Harris and Opong were spectacular in their successes, but they are representative of hundreds of Ghanaian laymen who evangelized Ghana. Most of them were mission catechists, but many were entirely independent. We have records of several independent churches formed in the 1920's which give us some idea of what some of these other prophets must have been like.

A few years after Harris left southwest Ghana, a man named Jehu Appiah felt himself called to be a prophet. It is claimed that the prayer group which gathered around him experienced wonderful visions and miracles. The Methodist supervisor finally decided he would have to discipline Appiah for heterodoxy. Appiah and his followers formed their own religious society. They were directed in visions to take a special sabbath, so they refused to work with their neighbors on that day. Persecution followed, and they withdrew to form a religious colony, the *Musamo Disco Cristo* Church (MDCC) at Mazano.[31]

Also in the mid-1920's prophet Phillip Kyei led his little group of followers into the wild Ghanaian forest. They were reportedly pacifistic, anticommercial, nudist ascetics! They called themselves the Iota Mission, taking their name from Jesus' endorsement of the Old Testament, "Not one iota of the Law will pass away until all is fulfilled." [32]

Opoku lists three other sects formed in the 1920's: Ghana Believer's Church at Odobeng, the Faith Society (later *Ossa Madih* Church), and the Saturday Believers. No information has been published about the first two. Baeta tells us a little about the early years of the Saturday Believers. Although they did not separate themselves from the world like the MDCC and Iota Mission, they were apparently also an intense prayer fellowship with distinctive practices clustered around the charismatic personality of their leader.[33]

Medicine Shrines

In the 1930's social anthropologists noted that southern Ghanaians were importing a host of new deities from northern Ghana and other less modernized areas. The old gods that the first anthropologists had found were losing their power and popularity. These old gods, like the Ashanti river gods *Tano* and *Pra,* offered positive benefits, but the new "medicine" cults like *Tigare* and *Blekete* were distinguished by the protection they claimed to offer against witchcraft. Witchcraft was hardly a concern of Ghanaians when their beliefs were first recorded and the old gods were in their prime. Rattray, for example, only mentions witchcraft six times in his extensive studies of the Ashanti. But already by the 1930's it had become an almost universal concern in Ghana.

The increased prevalence of witchcraft in colonial Africa might be compared to the advent of widespread and fanatical concern about witches in Europe as the holistic Catholic world-view was crumbling at the close of the Middle Ages. It is also similar to the change in Navajo religion today in the southwest United States. The integrated Navajo cosmos is giving way to divergent opinions, and Navajo religion is becoming witch religion. Colonialism has similarly undermined the traditional west African view of the world.

The increased prevalence of witchcraft beliefs also seems to be related to the disruption of family life by wage labor and cocoa wealth. Individuals who draw salaries often resent kinship obligations that made better sense when large families farmed together. Cocoa has wrought havoc with the matrilineages of the forest region; since trees are traditionally passed from father to son, the switch from other crops to cocoa has rather suddenly loosened the economic basis of matrilineal affection. Witches are said to attack mainly (some people say only) members of their own families, so it seems likely that the increase in witchcraft was stimulated by stresses introduced to traditionally close families by a changed economy.

People come to the shrines to seek protection from witches and poison, cures from all sorts of diseases, and success at their jobs or in school — the whole gamut of common needs. The priest divines the cause of their problems and prescribes ritual and often herbal treatment. Many clients come for private help, but public sessions are also held several times a week. Amid drumming and dancing the spirit possesses his priest and speaks to supplicants through him. Fasting is sometimes, though not always, used to stimulate trance. People from the neighborhood, usually women, who attend these public sessions regularly and dance along with the priest, are often mildly entranced too.

A shrine may be financed by a prosperous man, often too young for status in the traditional system, or a chief and his elders may decide to bring in a powerful god to deliver their village from crisis. Somebody from the village, perhaps a man or woman who has shown himself prone to possession, is sent to the home shrine of the god to learn its rituals, study the techniques of entranced dancing under an experienced priest, and bring the "medicine" back home. The financier, priests, and

30

assistants can become very prosperous from fees and gifts if the god proves effective.

Although a priest will usually help strangers who have heard of the fetish's power, most shrines also have a permanent congregation. People join the fetish by "eating the medicine," perhaps a bite or two of kola, and promising to obey certain laws, often patterned after the Ten Commandments. The rules of *Tigare,* the most famous fetish of west Africa, as reported by Busia from its Takoradi shrine were:

1. Thou shalt not steal.
2. Thou shalt not covet thy neighbor's wife.
3. Honour thy father and thy mother.
4. Thou shalt not bear false witness against thy neighbor.
5. Love thy neighbor as thyself.
6. Thou shalt not administer medicine of noxious nature or poison.[34]

Many fetishes also forbid resort to other gods, charms, or supernatural agencies.

Usually there is an even smaller community of the priest's relatives, assistants, and a few people under extended treatment actually living in the priest's house. These people help the priest take care of the shrine and his daily affairs, and they are subject to his authority.

Few medicine cults have been popular long. The awe which new and foreign medicines command is soon lost and another god brought in. Also, a shrine's popularity depends heavily on the personality and purported powers of the priest, so that the death of a charismatic priest can lead to the decline of his shrine. Field found that almost all of the 29 shrines she observed in the mid-1930's had severely declined 20 years later.[35]

Another anthropologist, Jack Goody, explained it this way:

These shrines are always waxing and waning in importance. . . . One shrine becomes successful, another fades out. The inhabitants are very pragmatic about such things, as well as eclectic. If one shrine appears to be effective, they take it up. If it fails them, they drop it.[36]

If a small god does not grant a petition, the failure may be blamed on a sin or ritual error on the part of the supplicant:

> An alternative, for obvious reasons not found in monotheistic religions, is a rejection of the shrine in question and the resort to another supernatural agency. This appears to me to be one aspect of the mobility of the medicine shrines in West Africa; they are the gods who failed.[37]

High expectations were probably crushed frequently when Ghanaians were subjected to the unpredictable fluctuations of the international market and the uncontrollable decisions of the colonial government, perhaps resulting in what all observers agree was an increase in the importation of new gods during the colonial period.

Areas farthest removed from the influence of colonialism are thought to have the most powerful medicines, and shrine priests dress in the costume and practice the ritual of the "less civilized" people who first worshiped their god. Nevertheless, the shrines borrow ethical principles, organizational techniques, and some rituals from the churches. Fiawoo writes of one fetish:

> Members feel that they perform identical roles with the church and that the cult occupies the same status as the church. As one cult priest puts it: "We preach the same gospel from different pulpits." [38]

The medicine shrines started to become popular nearly as early as the missions, and no doubt many people in search of a new god tried both major options at once. The climax of the medicine shrine movement was coincidental, however, with the numerical stagnation of the churches. People tended to join a fetish instead of a church, and especially in the 1940's many apparently quit churches to join fetishes. Ward wrote of that period:

> One might ask whether Christianity itself could not provide modern Ashanti with the sense of security which neither the secular world nor the traditional world could give, but we have seen that the main needs of individuals were explanations and

justifications for the otherwise inexplicable vagaries of disease and economic forces, changing and often unsatisfactory family situations, and political uncertainty. . . . Partly because they lacked attractive audience participating ceremonies and did not admit of the employment of such traditional ritual techniques as spirit-possession and healing, and probably most of all because of their alien origin and continuing alien control, Christianity did not provide a sufficient rallying power in the service of social integration.[39]

Methodist figures indicate that the number of mission converts began to decelerate around 1930, and that the orthodox churches' growth has slowed somewhat since 1940.[40] This conclusion is confirmed by Ione Acquah, who reported after his survey of Accra in the mid-1950's that average church attendance was only half of the claimed adult membership, and that it was generally accepted that there had been a decline in church attendance.[41] Recent membership statistics are readily available for the Methodist Church and the Presbyterian Church of Ghana, both of the large Protestant groups. Together the two churches grew an average of 4.2% a year 1960−68,[42] perhaps a little more than the growth in the general population during that period.

Some of the deceleration in church growth was probably due to disillusionment with the colonial regime. Taxation, unpopular agricultural policies, inflation, and war shortages contributed to rising nationalism. Young men often resented the alleged cultural imperialism of the missionaries as national feelings mounted. Even the politically unaware must have been less enchanted by the colonial order and Christianity. There were more European Methodist missionaries in Ghana in 1940−50 than at any other time, but during that period the number of Ghanaian Methodists actually decreased.

The churches in the 1950's responded by cutting the number of expatriate staff. Previously there had been rather few national churches, and undoubtedly the new political climate hastened ecclesiastical independence. The major Protestant churches are now all self-sufficient. In 1968 there were only 14 expatriate missionaries in the Methodist Church and 17 in the Presbyterian

Church of Ghana, most of these not pastors but medical personnel.[43] Except for occasional gifts for special projects, the churches are completely self-supporting. Many urban services are in English, but the vernaculars are used wherever most worshipers know one of them. Even people who go to spiritual churches usually also attend orthodox churches; the erudition of the orthodox ministers is certainly a reason. The spiritual churches have so far had to depend on established churches for the education and long-term nurture of their members. Most important, the spiritual churches have apparently won few of their members from non-Christian backgrounds; 42 percent of the Ghanaian population called themselves Christians during the 1960 census,[44] and the established churches can take credit for virtually all of this evangelization.

Orthodox leaders are themselves aware, however, that the established churches were slow to achieve independence from their missions and that they remain too European in character to this day. The missionaries, of course, had trouble separating Christianity and their own culture, and the African ministers who now lead the orthodox churches were for the most part reared in European-imitative homes so that their religious sensibilities are no longer the same as those of most Ghanaians. They are now looking seriously at the spiritual churches. They object to much that they see, but a growing number of established church leaders recognize that the spiritual churches have found Christian answers to some Ghanaian problems.

Meanwhile, the shrines are still a formidable force in Ghanaian religious life, and the use of herbalism and traditional psychiatric techniques in combination with modern science and organization, as envisioned by some of the leaders of the Traditional and Psychic Healing Association, may eventually revive the shrines' earlier dynamism. It is generally agreed among observers, however, that the medicine shrines have been losing their popularity since the late 1950's. Instead, the spiritual churches have been on the rise.

CHAPTER TWO

Spiritual Churches

Growth 1950—60

Beginning in about 1950 a few new spiritual churches were started each year in Ghana. By 1955 there were 11 indigenous spiritual churches, 3 African churches of Nigerian origin, and 3 independent non-Pentecostal Ghanaian churches in Accra. The total membership claimed by these churches was 4,500, a little over 2% of the city's population.[1]

The Apostolic Revelation Society, founded in 1945 by Prophet Wovenu, was among the first modern spiritual churches. Wovenu built a church and a school in his village. He placed himself under Presbyterian supervision for six years, but when his superiors told him to charge fees instead of allowing children to come to his school free, he withdrew. Wovenu has the power of healing, and is in many respects similar to earlier prophets like Harris, Opong, and Appiah. But the Apostolic Revelation Society is a larger, more formal organization, and the modern educational complex at the church's headquarters is a feat no earlier prophet would have attempted.[2]

The first president of Ghana, Kwame Nkrumah, also made crucial contributions to the development of spiritual churches. He borrowed Christian symbolism and the trappings of African prophetism, as well as Communist rhetoric, to build a "political religion" around himself. He had been a Protestant minister in the United States, but returned to his own country preaching, "Seek ye first the political kingdom and all things will be added to you." [3] He proclaimed himself *Osagyefo* ("Redeemer") and

35

promised an earthly "paradise in 10 years." The *Evening News* compared Nkrumah to Jesus; already at Christmas 1951 a journalist wrote of Nkrumah's birth:

> Angels were singing "the Messiah is coming" when in 1909 at Nkroful a woman was laboring to bring forth the Apostle of Freedom.[4]

The Young Pioneers, the party's youth, were taught to chant:

> Nkrumah is always right.
> Nkrumah is our Messiah.
> Nkrumah never dies.
> If you follow him, he will make you
>   fishers of men.[5]

This fantastic self-glorification and freewheeling syncretism were palatable to many Ghanaians because they are so much a part of the tradition of prophetism. Nkrumah combined science and technology with continued attention to charms, soothsayers, animal sacrifices, and magic. He was at once progressive and proud of his cultural heritage. He caught the imagination of many young men in Ghana, and the Nkrumah style — boldness, accomplishment, even greater ambition — is readily discernible in the religious regimes of some contemporary prophets.

The spiritual church movement began to gain momentum in the late 1950's. During the 1960 census 140,000 people, or 1.5% of the total urban and rural population, classified themselves as "African Christians." This did not include another 2.5% who called themselves "Apostolics."[6] Since the status value of spiritual church membership is still lower than that of orthodox membership, most people at any spiritual church service, if asked, will say they are Methodist or Presbyterian. So the 140,000 are only the faithful few from each spiritual church who no longer attended their former church, not the hundreds of thousands more who maintained dual membership, visited a prophet occasionally for advice and prayer, or sought out a spiritual church in times of personal trouble. By the end of the 1950's the movement was obviously well under way.

Nigerian Influence

Two foreign influences converged in Ghana in the 1950's to catalyze the indigenous spiritual church movement. The first was the immigration of thousands of Nigerians, mostly Yoruba, and the introduction of their prayer churches. The 19th and early 20th century African independent churches in Nigeria became much larger than their counterparts in Ghana; they expanded during the consolidation of colonial rule in the areas where the missions were most poorly staffed. Prayer groups appeared in both Nigeria and Ghana in the 1920's; in the 1930's, however, these prayer groups grew into mass churches in Nigeria, while they remained numerically insignificant in Ghana. The prayer churches developed large, sophisticated organizations capable of propagating Christian prophetism in Nigeria much earlier than in Ghana.[7]

There have been a few Nigerians in Ghana since the beginning of the century, but the number increased fourfold in the years 1948−60! Most of these immigrants were Yoruba, the tribe which has been most active in forming independent churches in Nigeria.[8] Nigerians brought their prayer churches to Ghana. Christ Apostolic Church had already arrived in Accra by 1938. The first Cherubim and Seraphim congregation was formed in 1949, the first Church of the Lord (Aladura) mission in 1953.[9]

These churches dealt directly with religious concerns shared throughout west Africa. They became popular among Ghanaians, too, and soon Ghanaians were being trained in Nigeria and Sierra Leone to be prayer church pastors. These churches are at best loosely organized, and schism has always been frequent among them. In Ghana, too, many of the prophets they trained led their congregations to break with the central headquarters in Nigeria. Other men simply observed Nigerian-trained prophets in action and founded their own churches after that pattern.

American and British Influence

Various missions from small churches in the United States and Great Britain constitute the other foreign strand woven into the Ghanaian spiritual church movement. Most of these missions derive from revivalistic Protestantism, notably Pentecostalism, and they have proved popular in Ghana. They maintain much of the fervor and theology of missionaries who came to Ghana in the early 19th century, and some of them reflect the influence Afro-Americans have had on revivalistic Protestantism since then.

Presbyterian and Methodist missions, in Ghana before mid-19th century, were joined by the Roman Catholics in 1880, the Seventh Day Adventists and AMEZ in 1898, the Anglicans in 1904, and the Salvation Army in 1911, so that Western Christianity had clearly displayed its divisions to Ghana already by that time. Revivalistic, fundamentalist groups began arriving in force in the 1920's: Faith Tabernacle, First Century Gospel, Jehovah's Witnesses, and Assemblies of God. This last group is Pentecostal, but speaking in tongues was apparently first introduced to an indigenous church by a missionary from Britain's Apostolic Church who arrived in 1937. The Southern Baptists began work in 1947, followed by their spiritual cousins in Baptist Mid-Mission and by Wycliffe in 1950.[10]

More and more missions arrived after Ghana's independence, because all the publicity Ghana's independence received in the United States brought Africa, particularly Ghana, to the attention of mission-minded Americans. About as many missions, all of them from the United States, have begun work in Ghana since independence as in the entire century before! Some of the new missions worked in north Ghana, still largely unevangelized, and among neglected immigrants from Nigeria and other neighboring nations. Others of the new missions, believing themselves bearers of a purer gospel, competed vigorously with established churches.

Revivalistic missionaries had no trouble believing in Africa's spirit powers, but they claimed to be able to summon an even greater Spirit through Christ. Their churches were places where a man could complain about his stomachache before the throne of Almighty God and hope for supernatural help. They were informal and emotional. In some churches people clapped and

38

sang lustily, in some there were healing miracles, and members of the Pentecostal groups spoke in strange tongues—all familiar elements of medicine shrine piety, but now justified with quotations from the Bible, an added attraction, especially for the newly literate. The new missions, especially the Pentecostal churches, continued to grow after the older missions had stopped. With the Aladura they provided models for indigenous churches and training for many would-be prophets.

The flood of 20th-century missions has catalyzed the indigenous church movement, not only in Ghana but throughout Africa. The number of Protestant missions from North America alone increased fourfold in the years 1930—60, and nearly half of these came from fundamentalist and Pentecostal groups.[11] Missionaries from the Christian Catholic Apostolic Church in Zion, whose headquarters are near Chicago, Ill., set off the spectacular prophetist movement of South Africa; the kinds of groups that are called "spiritual churches" in Ghana are even called "Zionist churches" in South Africa.[12] Several prominent indigenous churches in Kenya branched off from a Canadian Pentecostal mission.[13] Malawi has been the hotbed of the independent church movement in central Africa partly because of one missionary there, Joseph Booth, who personally helped form seven different denominations.[14]

The Nigerian prayer churches discussed in the previous section were themselves influenced by American and British missions. One of the earliest prayer societies depended on literature and letters from Faith Tabernacle in Philadelphia, Pa., and took that name as its own. A schism in Philadelphia gave rise to the First Century Gospel Church, and also resulted in Faith Tabernacle of Nigeria severing all its ties with Philadelphia. Instead they sought out a new relationship with the Apostolic Church, headquartered in Wales. Faith Tabernacle had stressed faith healing and had allowed for inspiration through dreams and visions, but it was Apostolic Church missionaries who taught Nigerian Christians to speak in tongues. Faith Tabernacle, later renamed Christ Apostolic Church, continues to stress the importance of speaking in tongues, and the practice

39

has filtered into other Nigerian prayer churches.[15]

The Apostolic Church has influenced indigenous churches in Ghana more than any other revivalistic mission. The beginning of its work in Ghana was remarkably similar to the situation in Nigeria. An indigenous church, which had been in correspondence with Faith Tabernacle, turned to the Apostolic Church after Faith Tabernacle's schism. The Apostolic Church sent a missionary to Ghana, but, as in Nigeria, many of the African Christians disapproved of the Apostolic Church for allowing the use of Western medicine. The local church in Ghana dismissed the missionary, and he formed a second, equally popular "Apostolic Church." In the 1950's a new alliance between this church and a Pentecostal group in the United States brought tension and then division from Apostolic Church officials in England. Both the churches that resulted have suffered several more schisms since then. Pentecostalism has, at least in this case, shown itself as decentralized and fissiparous as Ghana's own polytheistic shrines.

The Apostolic Church was originally invited to Ghana by a local congregation. One major schism in the Apostolic Church began when local leaders sought the support of an American mission. This is part of a recurring pattern: initiative by indigenous church leaders in drawing new missions to Ghana. Two early examples of this approach in Ghana, the AMEZ and the National Baptist Church, seem to have been little more than tools for tapping financial resources in the United States. All the more recently arrived missions whose history I have traced were lured to Ghana in nearly the same way.

The Mennonite Mission Board was approached in 1957 by the Ghanaian pastor of several dissident congregations which wanted to be Mennonite. When missionaries arrived, however, they found he had promised his followers mission hospitals and schools. After the missionaries revealed how little material aid they had to offer, most of the would-be Mennonites scattered. The missionaries remained to shepherd these crippled congregations. In 1969 they came into closer contact with indigenous churches through the ministry of the Rev. E. J. Weaver. Weaver set up Bible classes for spiritual church leaders and worked quietly toward reconciliation between orthodox and spiritual churches.[16]

The Lutheran Church—Missouri Synod started its mission in Ghana at the same time as the Mennonites. A dissatisfied AMEZ pastor had written all the many Lutheran churches in the United States, saying he had decided Luther's teachings were best. He sent pictures of his congregations and asked for help. The Missouri Synod salaried this man. His congregations hoped for a building program too, and they dispersed just as quickly as the Mennonite congregations had when they were disillusioned. Missouri Synod missionaries continued to lead small congregations and have found other opportunities for ministry. Lutheran leaders have been working closely with a spiritual church in Tema and helped form the Good News Training Institute, a new Bible school for spiritual church leaders growing out of Weaver's work.

I talked with a young Ghanaian who claimed to have invited the Christian Church to Ghana. He and some friends had led their own church until they succeeded in getting Christian Church missionaries to Ghana in 1966. Since that time the missionaries have split into two factions, each party receiving support from different congregations in the United States. The missionaries have established a clinic, an agricultural station, and a seminary. The young man was rightly proud to have drawn so much aid to Ghana, and when we talked he was making plans to study in the United States with the support of two American congregations.

Missions introduced since independence are, like the indigenous churches, small and numerous. A list would include the Mennonites, Lutherans, the Christian Church, the Universal Christian Church, two different groups called the Church of Christ, the Church of God, the Watchtower Church of the Delivering Christ, and the United Pentecostal Church. Most of them seem to have been invited to Ghana by indigenous churches, some are drawing their members and ministers from indigenous churches, and several are cooperating with indige-

41

nous churches in evangelism and education.

On the other side, the most successful indigenous church leaders have all had some contact with American Christianity. Several successful spiritual churches have reportedly received grants from groups in the United States. Given the low standard of living and restrictions on the use of foreign reserves, it is difficult even for a rich man to travel from Ghana, but Jehu Appiah of the MDCC and Yeboa-Korie of Eden have corresponded with Americans, hosted them in Ghana, and made trips to the United States. Virtually every spiritual church leader I met had plans—or at least hopes—to go to the United States.

The spiritual churches of Ghana are genuinely indigenous, but they are involved in a web of relationships with revivalistic Protestants elsewhere in Africa and the world. Trance and glossolalia were part of traditional Ghanaian religion, but their introduction into indigenous Christian worship is perhaps the most important influence missionaries from Britain and America have had within the spiritual church movement. Relationships between American missions and spiritual churches have multiplied during the last decade or two, and in the process a number of spiritual churches have become less syncretistic, more Bible-oriented, more American in organizational style. Spiritual churchmen have been surprisingly successful, however, in getting help from the United States without changing their doctrine or practice very much, because American Christianity is disorganized and some of its most active mission supporters are naive about contemporary Africa.

Growth 1960—70

During the 1960's, particularly in the last half of the decade, the spiritual church movement grew tremendously. It would be easier to measure this growth if it were simply a matter of people transferring their membership from one organization to another, but many orthodox church members also frequent spiritual churches and shrines. Perhaps someone who used to attend church and visit a shrine in time of crisis now goes regu-

42

larly to a spiritual church but also attends his former church several times a month. Another person who used to go to church several times a year and frequented shrines more often now goes to a spiritual church as his first resort, but, if that is unsuccessful, to a shrine. The result of these complicated individual changes is that the numbers attending spiritual churches are rapidly swelling, while both orthodox churches and the shrines are losing popularity.

The *Musamo Disco Cristo* Church has membership statistics for nearly its entire history:

Date	Number of Members	Gain in Members
1925	795	
1930	1,185	390
1935	14,125	12,940
1940	19,124	4,999
1945	22,895	3,771
1950	30,722	7,827
1955	35,516	4,794
1960	37,048	1,532
1965	41,271	4,223
1970	52,573	9,302

These records are another indication that the spiritual church movement made exceptional gains numerically during the late 1960's. More members were gained in 1965 – 70 than for all but one of the preceding five-year periods.[17]

No one knows the exact number of spiritual churches in Ghana. In 1962 several of the more prominent spiritual church leaders formed the Pentecostal Association of Ghana. It was modeled after the Christian Council of Ghana, which includes all the established orthodox churches. It was intended to encourage spiritual churches to learn from each other and to speak together on certain issues. The Association has been torn since its inception by rivalries among prophets. It now claims a membership of 100 churches representing 200,000 people.

In 1968 some less well-known spiritual church leaders organized the Ghana Council for Liberal Churches and managed to get government recognition. The official approval was good publicity, and it has allowed them to hold funds for distribution to worthy evangelists and to set up a pension plan for old prophets. They now claim a membership of 125 churches.

Many more churches are not tied to either national organization. They are hidden away in every corner of the big cities. Not all prophets have signboards, and some small groups may be unknown even to neighbors a few hundred yards away. Even in a small town informants will differ on the number of local spiritual churches. But everybody is agreed: in the past few years the movement has exploded in popularity, and there are suddenly hundreds of new spiritual churches in Ghana.

PART II

Eden Revival Church

CHAPTER THREE

Eden's History

The focus of this section is one church: its growth, teachings, piety, worship, community life, and the sorts of people who give it a unique character. This detailed case study of Eden Revival Church should yield insight into the character of the entire movement and, it is hoped, give a livelier, more personal and realistic understanding of spiritual churches in Ghana than statistics and generalizations.

Eden Revival Church is one of the most important of the new spiritual churches. People in many parts of the country have heard of it, thousands have been in some way touched by it, and many lesser churches in Ghana try to imitate it. Eden's founder and leader, the Rev. Brother Charles Yeboa-Korie, certainly among the most dynamic men in Ghana, is a particularly creative personality within the spiritual church movement. The history of Eden Revival Church not only reflects the rest of the movement but points toward the future of spiritual churches, in fact of all Christianity, in Ghana.

The Leader's Story

Within a few days of my arrival Yeboa gave me the following account of his call to the ministry. I was to hear the story several times again, since he often recounts parts of it to introduce himself, particularly to foreigners. This almost standard account of Eden's beginnings is not at all complete; only those incidents which legitimize Eden and Yeboa are recalled. Nevertheless, it reveals the church's historical self-understanding.

In Yeboa's account, he was a lay preacher in Methodist and Presbyterian churches until he realized that the ministers in those churches were not really following the Bible. He was especially disappointed that they failed to pray for his mother during her fatal illness. He read in the Bible that the God of Abraham, of Moses, of Joshua, of Jesus, and of the early church was a God who could heal, so he asked himself, "Is the Bible just a bunch of fairy tales?" He questioned Protestant clergymen and was surprised to hear that the first men sent from the Basel Mission Society to Ghana had come with "power." Yeboa reasoned that the Presbyterian Church was losing popularity in Ghana because the Spirit of its founders had been lost.

Yeboa began a 40-day fast, praying and visiting other spiritual churches. They were healing people, but he saw that they were falling into all sorts of unbiblical practices because they were ignorant. He began preaching for them, and soon he could heal too. He was at this time applying for a passport to go to the United States and study medicine. He had already been given a scholarship. He was teaching at Begoro, but was staying with a friend in Nsawam, a town near Accra, while waiting for his passport to be processed.

During his epic fast Yeboa had a crucial series of visions. A man carrying a Bible appeared to him on three consecutive nights. The first night Yeboa tried to heal people as a medical doctor, but he had time for only a few patients. The second night he preached to a large crowd about God's power to heal. The man showed him how to heal more people than he could touch by throwing water out over the crowd. Thousands were healed that night in his vision. The third night the man simply asked, "Which is better?" The answer was obvious to Yeboa, and the little group which was already coming to him for Bible study was urging him to stay in Ghana. A few days before he was supposed to leave for the United States, he decided to stay and be "God's man."

The Bible study group organized big meetings, and people came from all over Ghana to hear Yeboa. As the group became larger, they began to pressure him to give them a name. At first he refused because he was young and did not feel prepared to lead a church. He intended his group to be a prayer fellowship; his followers could join one of the established churches, too. Finally he acceded and gave his group a name. It was revealed to him in another vision. He saw the words "Garden of Eden," surrounded by flowers and fruit. Crowds of people were converging on a church there. He heard a woman's voice, "We must return again to the site of our first sin and repent." So he named the group "Garden of Eden," changed within a few months to "Eden Revival Church."

Most spiritual church leaders tell stories of a divine call similar to this history that Yeboa usually recounts. Odiyifo Dampreh, head of the Universal Prayer Group, tells of a vision of angelic light; the call was confirmed by two other people, but he tried to escape his vocation until God made him blind to teach him obedience.[1] Freeman, leader of the Pentecostal Church, began speaking in tongues and seeing visions when he visited the Church of the Lord (Aladura); he was committed to a mental hospital, but some friends in the Aladura congregation rescued him, prayed about him, and decided to send him to Nigeria for training as a minister. He told me that he left the Church of the Lord (Aladura) later when he learned more about the Bible. Jehu Appiah, founder of the *Musamo Disco Cristo* Church, saw three angels placing a heavenly crown on his head. Shortly thereafter another prophet arrived with the message, "Master Appiah, God has made you a great king." Finally Appiah saw a vision of an angel coming to him with an open Bible, and from that time on he began to do miracles.[2]

The heavenly vision, Biblical legitimation, and confirmation of the call by other Christians are common elements in all these accounts. These stories are history seen with the eyes of faith. It was difficult to search out more mundane strands in Eden Revival Church's development. From some early members of the church, occasional comments by Yeboa, and traces of documentation, I was able to piece together a more complete history.

Prophet, Prayer Group, and Church

Yaw Charles Yeboa-Korie was born in the village of Asonafo in Akim Abuakwa in 1938. His father died early, and since his family was poor, he was reared by a teacher at his primary school. His childhood seemed harsh. He recalls having to plait the women's hair and carry grain. His stepparents ate meat themselves but would not share it with him. They gave him a woman's cloth for school, but otherwise he had tattered clothes. Even though he had to do chores all his spare daytime hours, he excelled in school by studying late at night. Sometimes he would stay awake and cry during the night; it was sadness, he says, that led him to start fasting. He remembers walking down a lonely bush road thinking:

> Shall I be a doctor and heal many people? Shall I be a preacher and teach crowds of people? Shall I be a statesman, perhaps prime minister?

Other people who knew him as a boy say he was studious, quiet, and shy, sometimes locking himself alone in his room for hours.

Yeboa was an outstanding student in secondary school at Abuakwa State College. He was a champion sportsman, representing Ghana internationally in track and field. Plagued by "times of constant illnesses which could not be diagnosed," he began intensive Bible study, fasting, and visits to various prayer groups.

Yeboa began to perform healings; his first miracle, as he recounts it, took place on the way to a prayer meeting:

> On one of my usual visits to a Spiritual Group, I encountered a sick man. Then, all of a sudden, I felt there was a Spirit force working on me. When I laid my hands on the man and prayed for him, the latter suddenly started wallowing in an unconscious state on the ground. When he ceased rolling, he openly testified that his sickness had disappeared.[3]

48

At this same time he began volunteer preaching at some Presbyterian and Methodist churches.

He taught for a few years after sixth form of secondary school, and he became assistant headmaster of the secondary school in Begoro. Occasionally he advised his students on the basis of visions he had seen about them. He preached for two local prayer groups. He had a vision of bringing a dead man to life by surrounding him with candles; the man rose, placed one of the candles above his head, and praised God. The very next day a man who was critically ill, nearly dead, was brought to him; Yeboa followed his vision, and, as in the vision, the man got up, held the candle above his head, and praised God. Brother Yeboa used this method of healing from that time until 1968.

In 1962 Yeboa moved to Nsawam to prepare for emigration. The little group that was to become Eden began one afternoon when he noticed a girl on the street. He mentioned to a friend that he "saw" that she was being troubled by dreams and would someday be found dead in her room unless she were helped. The friend rushed to the girl and told her what Yeboa had seen. She had not, in fact, been able to sleep because of ugly mice that appeared to her in the night. Yeboa hinted that there was witchcraft in the house. He gave her a blessed handkerchief and water, which stopped the dreams, and he moved into the house himself. No one had been able to stay there for long, except one old woman. Vultures and snakes reportedly used to wander through the house. Yeboa dared to live there and began holding prayer meetings in the house. The girl he had cured and three of her young friends, a 17-year-old boy, and later two older men joined Yeboa several times a week for Bible study and prayer.

Eden's beginnings are typical of spiritual churches in Ghana. Some churches are started by young men, unemployed and eager to do the Lord's or anybody else's work, who seek the special abilities expected of prophets as assistants in established spiritual churches and eventually found sects of their own. But many leaders, like Yeboa, are brought in contact with the movement because of illness and are surprised to receive visions and the gift of effective prayer as well as their own health. It is not unusual in Ghana for pious Christians, either as individuals or with prayer circles, to pray for others in need. If one or two sudden cures are reported, someone like this may be swamped by supplicants.

In a pamphlet prepared for the Presbyterian Church of Ghana, Ntiforo and Rutishauser described how a spiritual church usually evolves out of such a situation:

> People who have found help with a leader continue to come to him, not only when they are in need, but also for regular worship. They attach themselves to him and desire to live near him and even with him, and thus form the nucleus of a congregation.[4]

This is precisely what happened in the case of Eden.

One of the girls in the prayer group was a nurse at the local hospital, and if the doctors failed to help a patient, she sometimes recommended Yeboa. Other people came for help from Nsawam, Begoro, Oda, and even Kumasi. So many were being healed that they had to move their services to an open place. Yeboa was a more timid preacher then, but he taught the Bible carefully. They had some drums and a homemade one-string bass. They met all day Wednesday and from about three o'clock in the afternoon until long after midnight on Saturday.

Yeboa and the woman in the house who was suspected of being a witch quarreled one day in the street, and Yeboa was charged with breach of peace. He feels the judges of the case were biased. He was put in prison briefly for contempt of court. The case dragged on for half a year before he was acquitted. The unintended result of the litigation was publicity for the young healer in Nsawam, and crowds of people came from Accra to see him. Yeboa then heeded his vision and decided against going to the United States.

Again, Ntiforo and Rutishauser's description of the typical spiritual church fits Eden perfectly:

> The leader of a powerful prayer group will soon have a number of helpers: assistants in worship, keepers of the house, etc. As this "ministry" develops, the organization grows: these helpers must be given some share in the income and the government of

the group; this is often done in a very paternalistic way, not really curtailing the power of the leader. . . . A not unimportant step is the selection of a name. Names like *Jesus Garden,* Bethlehem *Camp,* Prayer *Circle,* Prayer *Society,* Power *House* of Prayer, etc. show that the word church is avoided, but later given by the people.[5]

Ntiforo and Rutishauser argue that charismatic leaders almost always resist formal organization, but that their adherents begin to demand the structures they enjoyed in their former churches: a youth group, choir, women's fellowship, church almanacs, and calendars. Yeboa confirms that he did not want his group to become a church. He gave the group a name only because they insisted, and then instead of calling it a church, he originally named it "*Garden* of Eden."

When Yeboa finally decided to organize his followers into another spiritual church, he used the money he had saved for his trip to the United States to build a church shed. Since most of the people who came to him for prayers were traveling from Accra, he built the shed in Mamprobi, a suburb of Accra. During this period Yeboa often retreated to a mountain place for prayer. Sometimes he would not speak to people at all, communicating with those around him only with written messages. He fasted several times for 40 days, once for 60 days.

Eden services were held on Wednesday and Saturday, often lasting until the early hours of the morning. Yeboa sometimes dressed in white like a doctor. Incense was burned, and his patients would be doused with water. They would be surrounded, one after another, by a corps of nurses holding candles, and Yeboa would pray for each of them. Wonderful miracles were reported, and although regular members were few, Eden's crowds overflowed by the hundreds into the streets.

Modernizing Eden

Although extraordinarily popular and reputedly powerful, Eden must have been similar in style to other spiritual churches in Ghana until 1966. Its development—first a charismatic healer, then a small prayer group with him, and finally a larger, loosely organized healing cult—was characteristic of spiritual churches.

Then in the summer of 1966 Yeboa traveled to the United States for three months. He went with the new government's blessing to woo more American mission support for Ghana. He failed in that, but returned with a bevy of new ideas and proceeded to make Eden into a new-style spiritual church that was later to become a model for many other Ghanaian churches.

He oriented Eden toward evangelism, adopting its present slogans, "Crossing Africa with Jesus," and "Eden Is Africa's Hope." He built a much bigger shed for the church in Kokomlemle, closer to downtown Accra. He bought striking uniforms for the choir, and brought the band, already grown from a homemade bass to a five-piece combo, to something like its present size. He hired musicians to train the new choir and band. He bought the short-lived Eden Poultry Farm and founded a private elementary school, later secondary and commercial schools, to provide funds for evangelistic crusades. Eden launched branch churches in Kumasi and Begoro with evangelistic crusades, and tiny Eden congregations involving secondary school students in Aburi and Ghanaian university students in London were started.

In 1968 several open-air services were held in Accra, and Eden opened branches in Akwamufie, Winneba, and Nkawkaw. The church published an occasional magazine, first called the *Edenian,* later the *Torch.* Many people no longer felt the need to supplement Eden with worship in an orthodox church, so the Saturday night service was moved to Sunday morning. Yeboa began wearing a coat and tie, sometimes even a clerical collar, to Sunday services. In the spring he ordained several junior pastors.

All of these changes were part of a conscious attempt to create a unique church. Yeboa borrowed heavily from Ghanaian spiritual churches, orthodox established churches, and American Pentecostal churches, but much of his pioneering was pure innovation. He helped start the Ghana Pentecostal Association in 1963 and was glad when other spiritual church leaders borrowed his ideas. In describing the anniversary meeting of the Association in 1968, the editor of the *Torch* commented:

> It became quite clear that the Spiritual Churches were not going to be satisfied any longer with the old, unorganized Ghana Apostolic tradition of gathering a few Mames and children, acquiring an old double-bass, and merely shouting away into the night. . . . The various choirs and singing bands representing their churches were elaborately and neatly dressed, and they showed in their singing that they had come under sound training. . . . Indeed, it became crystal clear that the Pentecostal Revolution which Bro. Yeboa-Korie started in the Eden Revival Church in 1966 was spreading like wildfire throughout Ghana.[6]

Only one other spiritual church, Dr. Blankson's Bethany Church, rivals Eden in the craft of combining American slickness and sophistication with the effectual fervor of "mames and children . . . shouting away into the night." A number of other spiritual churches, however, are trying to copy what they can of Eden's band and choir, financial strength, and expansiveness.

During the last several years Eden hosted a number of foreign missionaries. Paula Jackson, a white American evangelist, was in contact with Eden almost from its beginning and worked full time for Yeboa after 1965. She helped arrange his visit to Philadelphia, Pa., in 1966. On his own initiative he went from there to Oklahoma and tried to meet with T. H. Osbourne, a famous Pentecostal preacher. Paula Jackson became more and more involved in Eden, finally evangelizing for the church in Begoro in 1968.

In October 1968 she was joined briefly by a black American, Stephen Williams, a member of the National Baptist Convention, sponsored by several independent churches in Philadelphia. Williams was offended by Eden's use of handkerchiefs, blessed Bibles, water, olive oil, candles, and incense. He was convinced that people thrown on the ground in church were possessed by "other spirits." He doubted whether many Edenians had been "born again," and regretted their lack of "Spirit baptism" and speaking in tongues. The doctrinal clash, compounded by personal conflicts, finally convinced the American Pentecostals that Eden was demonic. Williams told me that Yeboa had predicted on his arrival that he would be gone by December, and, in fact, he and Paula Jackson left after an unexpected quarrel on Nov. 30. Shortly thereafter a minister whose church was supporting Paula Jackson came to Ghana. Eden stopped using incense and candles publicly shortly before his arrival, probably an attempt to attract American funds.

Yeboa visited other churches in Germany, England, and New Jersey in July 1969. Several Europeans and Americans are working for Eden now, mainly as teachers in the church and schools. My invitation to do research and teach part time in Eden was part of an ongoing interest in getting assistance and establishing contacts abroad.

Eden is moving closer and closer toward the orthodox churches. Although Eden still belongs to the Pentecostal Association of Ghana, it is not now a very active member because of "petty quarreling" and "jealousy" among the various spiritual church leaders. In late 1970 Eden Revival Church became the first spiritual church to become a member of the Christian Council, the organization of established, orthodox churches in Ghana. Yeboa thinks the older denominations in Ghana will soon adopt healing, and he sees Eden as a bridge between the spiritual and orthodox churches.

Yeboa is still "building a foundation." A large orchestra, with a drama and choral group, is being trained. In late 1970 a more democratic church organization was established, including a synod, council, and regional councils. In 1971 the Eden Church Secretariat, headed by J. R. Anquandah, published the *Eden Revival Church of Ghana Handbook.* It included Eden's first formal creedal statement, which echoes the Apostles' Creed, the Nicene Creed, and Reformation statements of faith more clearly than do most of the sermons I heard.

Eden Revival Church has evolved from a prayer group, through the old style of spiritual church, to a dynamic, unique organization. Yeboa would like to evangelize not only throughout Ghana but in the rest of Africa and the world. He hopes that African religiosity, if turned toward Christ, would be contagious in Europe and the United States. It is probable that Eden Revival Church, having combined some of the strengths of both spiritual and orthodox churches, will significantly influence the whole Christian movement at least in Ghana.

Eden in National Politics

The spiritual church movement is the cultural counterpart of political nationalism. The spiritual churches, like the political nationalist movement, involve all sectors of society, but are led by educated young men. Spiritual churches are at once traditional and progressive, just as political independence involves both an assertion of African worth and an embrace of Western culture. Since churches like Eden were, in part, spawned by nationalism and are similar to the independence movement in so many ways, one might expect them to be especially nationalistic. Yet Eden's relationship to the government of Ghana's first president, Kwame Nkrumah, and to his ideals was ambiguous.

In April 1965 Nkrumah's party newspaper, the *Evening News,* accused Yeboa of being a tyrannical, subversive quack in an article entitled "Exploiters in the Name of the Church" (April 10, 1965):

In EDEN REVIVAL "CHURCH" which styles itself as an autonomous state within the State, "Prophet" Yeboah Korie thinks he can override the laws of Ghana when he assaults a member of his congregation just because "the Holy Ghost" has told him that Kojo, Afua or Esi possesses evil spirits. And yet these are the very people who fatten his banking accounts. . . . Eden Revival Church masquerading as a religious organization, has been the very receptacle for counter-revolutionary thoughts, where politics prejudicial to national security have taken the place of religious sermon.

The editorial attack was inspired by a member of parliament who had been helped by Yeboa but later became disgruntled. The articles were biased, so Yeboa posted them in church for all to read, and invited their author to make his charges publicly at an Eden service. He wanted people to compare the assertions to reality.

The article's charge of "counter-revolutionary" sermons in Eden may well have been somewhat factual. Since spiritual churches attract people in trouble, many of the people who were suffering during the Nkrumah years, potential subversives, came to Yeboa for help. This included high-ranking government officials who feared they might be victims of the political intrigue which characterized Nkrumah's latter years.

More important, most Edenians are Akans from cocoa country, and since Nkrumah's government appropriated about half the money from their sales through the Cocoa Marketing Board, opposition to Nkrumah was widespread and deep among Akans.[7] Yeboa himself is an Akan from Akim, and the paramount chief of Akim was Nkrumah's archenemy. Nkrumah neglected Akim in development plans, and in 1959 he finally deposed the chief. Yeboa had good reason to resent the government, and he tells with pride of secret maneuverings to reconcile two important Akan chiefs and thus strengthen the opposition to Nkrumah. Yeboa's political loyalty seemed questionable to the special security police, and after the newspaper editorial they sometimes sent agents to Eden's services. But even in 1970 when it was popular to pose as Nkrumah's foe, Yeboa said he always had told his people "to keep cool and obey."

Nkrumah himself heard about Yeboa's leadership abilities, and in late 1965 tried to convince him to study in the U.S.S.R., become a member of parliament, and use his oratorical skill to further the causes of socialist Ghana and Africa. This patriotic appeal must have been difficult for him to reject. Nkrumah, however, used all sorts of pagan "protection," and Yeboa says he refused to work for him unless he repented of his "idolatry." Also, by that time Nkrumah's future seemed insecure, and Yeboa was afraid to link Eden Revival Church too closely to Nkrumah's regime.

In January and February 1966 Yeboa held a series of "unity services" at a large theater in Accra. His sermons were printed in the Sunday *Mirror*. He called for reformation and reconciliation among Christians and for cordial relations between Moslems and Christians for the sake of African unity:

56

Colonialists divided mother Africa, breaking her supreme protective force, and started ruling her selfishly. And we ourselves have further divided her spiritual and physical force with our religions — Euro-Christian and Islamic religions featuring prominently among us. Appalling as it is, Africa's two main religions contest with one another, making man's common heritage valueless. Nay, the Christians, of which I am one, and can therefore be explicit about, have unduly divided themselves into schisms and sects.[8]

Yeboa sincerely holds these opinions, but they also echo themes from Nkrumah's propaganda. In the same issue the *Mirror* reported that top-ranking party members were urging religious unity.

The Rev. W. G. M. Brandful, secretary of the Christian Council, politely refused to "summon a continental conference at which every obstacle in the way of Church Unity should be swept away" and directed those seeking unity, not to "the friendship and protection of the powerful" but to the "power of sacrificial love." [9] Only the first in a series of articles by Brandful was published. Brandful thinks he was censored because he did not, like Yeboa, toe the party line. Yeboa says his intention was really to unite Christians, most of whom opposed Nkrumah, so that they could speak to the government together. Whatever the private motives for his "unity services" may have been, he certainly gave the impression of rallying behind Nkrumah.

In early 1966 Yeboa was afraid of being put in prison under the Preventive Detention Act, and his apparent support for Nkrumah may have been partly pragmatic. He began a 40-day fast at that time to ask for God's protection. On the night of the 37th day it is said Yeboa told one of the girls in the church that Nkrumah had been overthrown. The next day — Feb. 24, 1966 — the coup d'état occurred.

A group of junior army officers, the National Liberation Council, ruled Ghana for three years. Yeboa, like most Ghanaians, was relieved by the coup and was an enthusiastic, although not uncritical, supporter of the National Liberation Council.

The new government was helpful in arranging his trip to the United States in the summer of 1966; it wanted him to persuade American missionaries to evangelize, set up schools, and build hospitals in Ghana. The National Liberation Council also sold some of Nkrumah's infant socialist enterprises to foreign capitalists and increased imports from the United States. It retreated from Nkrumah's intense nationalism and moved Ghana much more into a neocolonial relationship with Europe and the United States. Yeboa's visits to the United States immediately after the coup and in 1968 should be understood in this context.

In late 1969 a new constitution went into effect. Three of the coup leaders continued to serve jointly as president, and their favorite candidate, Dr. K. A. Busia, was elected to the office of prime minister. Before independence in 1957 Dr. Busia had led the Opposition Party, which preferred gradual to immediate independence and federalism to national unity. Yeboa did not openly endorse any candidate until after the election. When a bomb exploded in Parliament Building just before the election, he preached a sermon on obeying the law. He privately favored Busia, sometimes made his preference known indirectly, and estimated that 80 percent of Eden's members voted for Busia. On the day Busia's electoral victory was announced, he led the entire church in Busia's party cheer. He told me later he wanted to avoid being partisan, but hoped that the entire nation would unite behind the new prime minister. When the new government issued its controversial alien expulsion order in December 1969, a decision which forced thousands of Nigerians and other Africans to leave the country, Yeboa expressed approval in a sermon.

In 1971, after my fieldwork, another coup ended Busia's government. The new regime, headed by Colonel Ignatius Kutu Acheampong, was radically nationalistic. It repudiated part of Ghana's foreign debt, delayed payment on the rest, and seized controlling interest in foreign-owned mining and timber companies. The resulting loss of international credit brought food shortages and high prices. In addition to this, martial rule also led to some internal disgruntlement. Fortunately for the regime,

58

however, the international price of cocoa doubled during their first year in power.

In summary, Yeboa has occasionally tried to influence the nation's course, but usually privately. Eden Revival Church has not been especially nationalistic. Although nationalism has been a prime factor stimulating the spiritual church movement, Eden Revival Church has tended to favor more moderate politics.

CHAPTER FOUR

Eden's Teachings

The teachings of Eden are primarily the teachings of Brother Yeboa, who spent several hundred hours graciously explaining his doctrines and beliefs to me. The Bible is the ultimate authority, but because Yeboa is thought to be especially guided by the Spirit, his interpretations are seldom questioned. The church changes as Yeboa's spiritual researches lead to new "discoveries." A few Edenian pastors have distinctive theologies, and I have tried to indicate these variations. Church members, especially those who do not attend regularly, have a less thorough understanding of Eden's doctrines, and if asked about their beliefs they frequently defer to Brother Yeboa.

Eden's message is basically twofold: law and power. Edenians say their church combines the best of both orthodox and spiritual churches. The orthodox churches preach morality but, according to Edenians, cannot save people in trouble. The spiritual churches are powerful, but ignorant; as J. R. Anquandah put it:

> They just play on people's emotions. They make Christ into as aspirin; take it, and when you feel better, forget it.

Yeboa has completed more years of school than any other spiritual church leader in Ghana, so while other prophets can offer emotional ritual and "faith healing," Yeboa is usually better at explaining the significance of these things and teaching Biblical morality.

Law

Although most of the people who listen to Yeboa come because they have heard he can do wonders, he says:

> I believe more in teaching than in healing. If you heal somebody, and he jumps up to steal, you haven't done much. If you heal somebody, and he jumps up to kill or commit adultery, you haven't done much.

Yeboa and a few disciples diligently search the Bible for moral guidance.

They are like the Congolese Protestants Andersson describes:

> The catechists display a particular fondness for the law. They are the servants of a Protestant Church, yet their preaching possesses a very legalistic quality. They often concentrate their teaching on the Ten Commandments. . . . The members of the the church do not protest against this legalistic preaching. On the contrary, they ask for new laws, new rules, new prohibitions. They want their whole life to be set within the framework of precise and detailed laws.[1]

God's laws are not grudgingly accepted as external constraints; obedience is joyful and enthusiastic. Edenians can say with the Psalmist:

> Teach me, O Lord, the way of Thy statutes;
>   and I will keep it to the end.
> Give me understanding, that I may keep Thy law
>   and observe it with my whole heart.
> Lead me in the path of Thy commandments,
>   for I delight in it (Ps. 119:33-35).

The grace of God is clearly depicted in Eden, but His judgmental attributes are more frequently mentioned. Yeboa argues that Christ did not come to destroy the Old Testament law but to make it more demanding and complex.

The legalistic tone of Eden's message echoes parts of the Bible, but also draws strength from the authoritarian character of many Ghanaian institutions. For example, small gods *(abosom)* are often praised because they have power to bring sickness or even death to those who disobey them. In comparison the God of the Christians sometimes seems lax and permissive.[2] Edenians seem to find reminders of God's wrath helpful in maintaining moral lives.

Many Edenians believe Yeboa is clairvoyant, so they feel, "God is watching everything I do." If someone has been disobedient, the Spirit may "beat" him in church. Women who have practiced witchcraft are sometimes thrown violently to the floor, rolling wildly until exhausted. One prominent Edenian told me, "If you couldn't demonstrate God's power, no one would obey Him." Death is the final demonstration of God's power, and the promise of heaven and threat of hell are often preached.

Obedience to those in authority is an important element in Eden's teaching. Children should obey parents, students should obey teachers, workers should obey employers, church members should obey church leaders, and citizens should obey the government. Edenians are encouraged to influence those in authority and, if a human authority contradicts God's laws, to disobey. Yeboa himself refused to do Nkrumah's bidding unless he reformed. This was a rare exception, however. The weight of Eden's message is for almost unquestioning obedience.

Obedience is thought to be a sort of social gospel. Africans, according to Eden's leadership, are especially wicked and in need of discipline. Through the worship of idols, it is argued, Africans have become divided and have fallen into habits which keep them from development:

> As a nation, Ghana should awake from the age-old hypnosis of superstitions, fears, misbeliefs, animism, idolatry, dishonesty, laziness, nepotism, superiority, etc. etc., for the establishment of different arts and sciences, culture and learning, a viable political rule and a living farming system. And as Christians,

Ghana should break through the lethargy which has dazed us from fighting the fetishes, idols, jujus, etc., the root cause of Africa's spiritual ills.[3]

J. R. Anquandah wrote:

The causes of Africa's problems are not far to seek. Compared to the average man of the Western world, the African is still, generally speaking, a lazy person. He still lacks a sense of responsibility. Above all he still lacks that "Something" which teaches the innermost self of a man and prompts him to give all of himself in order to help build a broken and divided nation. . . . That "Something" which guided Moses, David, Peter, Paul, and Jesus is Love.[4]

Advocacy of Christianity as a new basis for African society is reminiscent of Augustine's argument that Christianity had not undermined Rome but was actually a surer foundation for the Empire than traditional Roman customs and religion. If Yeboa can build the large evangelistic association he envisions, he believes he could transform Ghana, perhaps all of Africa, and pave the way for development.

Power

The Need for Power

Demonstrations of God's power are deemed necessary because the devil's power is already horribly real to Edenians. Along with most Ghanaians, they are troubled by witchcraft. It is believed that more than three-fourths of all women are witches, using the devil's power to "eat" others in their families spiritually and causing all sorts of diseases and ill fortune. A husband may watch his wife sleep quietly all night and still suspect she is hurting him; it is thought a witch's body rests deceptively in bed while her spirit rushes off to the forest to feast with other witches. It is said many women are witches and do not even know it. People are afraid to walk in lonely places at night, and many suffer nightmares, illness, and job loss because of suspected witchcraft in their families.[5]

Some Ghanaians believe that almost half of all men use spiritual poison. Envious men are said to poison their superiors at work, perhaps placing a special stick at a place where the enemy will pass or putting deadly powder in his food. Bad medicine like this can cause a man to lose his money, his health, or even his life. A friend of mine quit his job because he thought someone in the office was trying to poison him. Another man had to flee his village because he was under spiritual attack.

Most Ghanaians have some sort of "protection" against such things. They carry talismans, cover their faces with white powder, or rub some "medicine" into incisions on their skin, according to the advice of fetish priests, Moslem mallams, or some other "spiritual men."

Good and bad fortune are almost always attributed to spiritual forces. If a woman falls sick or is barren, she looks for a witch in her house. If there is an automobile accident, the devil is responsible. If a man is successful, it is because he has "something powerful behind him." Even if people take steps to deal with material causes of trouble, they usually try to get spiritual protection too.

The churches condemn both good and bad magic, the shrines that catch and punish witches as well as witches! Edenians believe, in fact, that the fetish shrines are the main cause of witchcraft, a complete reversal of the traditional opinion. They believe that the kindly men who prepare protective talismans are as much tools of the devil as the awful wizards. Libations poured to ancestors and homage to the spirits of the rivers, the ocean, mountains, and natural wonders are all labeled idolatry.

Just as early Christian fathers placed the pantheon of Mediterranean gods in hell, the comparatively young Christian community in Ghana believes that the Ghanaian spirits are still powerful but that they are all demonic. It is no wonder Edenians believe that the devil, not God, is now controlling the world. They recall how the devil tempted Jesus; he said all the kingdoms of the world were his to give (Luke 4:6). The dragon may have been thrown from heaven, but he will have, according to Yeboa, power over the earth until the millennium (Rev. 12:12).

Brother Yeboa often cites Ephesians:

> For we are not contending against flesh and blood, but against the principalities, against the powers, against the world rulers of this present darkness, against the spiritual hosts of wickedness in the heavenly places (Eph. 6:12).

Many orthodox Christians feel completely unprotected by God, so they sometimes use medicines and shrines secretly.

Yeboa, however, reassures his people of the Biblical faith in God's omnipotence. The high God created the universe, he preaches, so He must be more powerful than all other spirits. Again and again Edenians go back to the first few chapters of Genesis, and their praise is often centered around His work of creation. It is believed that God exercises His power fully after death, rewarding some and punishing others. The frailty of all human enterprise and the approach of death, especially the possibility of premature death, are Yeboa's constant themes.

He convinces Ghanaians of God's omnipotence most effectively by an ongoing demonstration of power. Moses and the prophets, Jesus and the apostles did wonders even greater than the devil is working in Ghana today. Their God was obviously powerful, but although modern Christians say they believe in Him, most of them do not dare ask for Him to do miracles. The Son of God was not only a teacher, but an exorcist and a healer. He showed His authority over demons, sickness, and nature. He saw the devil face to face and resisted temptation so He could finally say, "All power is given to Me in heaven and on earth" (Matt. 28:18). He told His followers, "He who believes in Me will also do the works I do; and greater works than these will he do, because I go to the Father" (John 14:12). They went out preaching Christ's power and doing miracles. The orthodox churches, it is said, teach these wonderful stories as if they were fables, denying God's power. But Yeboa boldly "believes the Bible like a fool," and daily demonstrates that faith in God is stronger than all of Ghana's awesome spirits.

There are two major ways in which he demonstrates Christ's power: effective prayer and supernatural knowledge.

Yeboa prays about the various problems people bring to him — unemployment, the danger of driving in Accra, lost money, a school examination, loneliness, a quarrel between husband and wife. Of course, not all these problems are solved, and regular members accept frustrations as God's way of trying and strengthening them. Eden's prayers for the sick, however, often are granted suddenly.

Yeboa fully appreciates the material causes of disease, takes modern medicine himself, sometimes prescribes it for his patients, and speaks well of hospitals and doctors. But it seemed that church members often waited much longer than seemed advisable to seek professional medical help. Yeboa teaches that the root cause of ill-health in Ghana is idol worship. Because Ghanaians have been "worshiping the devil" and sometimes even offering him human sacrifice, they have invited a legion of dirty spirits to their homes. "Every disease," according to Yeboa, "is at least in part spiritual." And it is believed possible to cure any disease through prayer.

Faith is the source of healing in Eden. In his private devotional notes Pastor Buabeng, pastor of Eden in Begoro, wrote:

How did God create? By the Word of Faith. He said, "Let there be." He created with words. Jesus knew the secret of words. He healed the sick with words. He raised the dead with words. He stilled the sea with, "PEACE be still." We become the sons of God, partakers of His very nature, by acting on words. We become faith men and women, we use faith words, and produce faith results.

Yeboa once explained to me that all his power is based on the assurance that comes from wrestling with Bible passages until he understands. Then he can preach with such force that many people will fall down if he just touches them. This wisdom leads to "what the people call power."

Yeboa and the other healers in Eden study various ways of bringing people to faith. In Pastor Buabeng's words:

The healer is the man who can inspire faith. The tongue may

65

speak to human ears, but souls are revealed by souls that speak to souls. He is the forceful man whose soul is large, and who can enter into souls, inspiring hope in those who have no hope, and faith in those who have no faith in God, in nature, nor in man.

Yeboa's calling card reads, "Reverend-Brother Charles Yeboa-Korie, God's Man of Faith and Power." He is, more than anyone else, the channel through which God's power flows to Edenians. He teaches that all Christians can heal in Jesus' name; Yeboa's assistants and pastors at outstations regularly exercise this gift. But repeated and prolonged fasting has supposedly given Yeboa exceptional power; when others fail, he may be able to help, because some demons cannot be driven out by anything but prayer and fasting (Mark 9:29). After long "research" Yeboa has mastered the "science of healing." If he does not attend a service in Accra, few Edenians come and only a handful are cured. When he went to the United States for a few months, the church almost went bankrupt. He refuses to be called "prophet" like some other spiritual church leaders, but he often compares himself to Moses and Elijah, Jesus and Peter, Luther and Wesley—powerful men through whom God moved His people to faith. Yeboa has to rebuke his followers again and again, "They try to make me a god."

Any point of contact with Yeboa can help heal. He told me once that if he were a doctor "people would be healed just by the way I would talk to them, by the way I would use my hands." If a pain does not disappear easily, Yeboa will nearly always handle his patient physically. Usually he presses his hand against the patient's forehead, stretching the neck backwards. This causes the person to fall back, and Yeboa is extremely skillful in suspending a person comfortably on his knee and free arm. He may massage the ailing member with olive oil or tell the patient to exercise it. People are sometimes healed if Yeboa only stands close to them. He splashes his patients with water, because people want to be touched before they will believe, and he can reach more people with water than with his hands. He argues that this is no different from Jesus' use of spittle in healing. (Mark 7:33)

When Yeboa prays for people, the Spirit often "catches" them as part of the healing process. Others are "caught" unexpectedly as they dance and sing or when they are splashed with water. Their bodies become tense, they quiver, and often their legs kick and arms swing spasmodically. If there is music, they may jump or roll as if given over to the rhythm. Sometimes a person simply collapses into Yeboa's arms. Then the nurses ease him to the floor, where he lies as if asleep, but with fists clenched and toes tensed, for five or ten minutes. Occasionally a person like this actually does pass on into sleep. People's faces always seem taut and troubled when they are caught, but the Spirit is said to help heal, and many people have told me they always feel better afterwards.

Trance in spiritual churches is markedly different from that in "fetish" shrines. A pagan priest takes on the personality of the god who seizes him, dances with some control for a long time under the spirit's influence, and communicates with those around him in the name of the god. In Eden the "priest" is never entranced. Those who are caught have brief, uncontrolled, private experiences.

Men are seldom caught; some of the women look forward to being caught, at least in a mild way, at every service. People who have been fasting are especially vulnerable. Yeboa says light-skinned people seem more prone to being caught than dark-skinned. People with "soft temperaments" fall most quickly, but those who resist fall most violently. Once in a great while someone will begin speaking in tongues, but this is considered disruptive and is never allowed to continue.

The same Spirit which catches the sick to heal them may seize the wicked to "beat" them. A person punished by the Spirit will twist and flail uncontrollably, perhaps pommeling his own body. A girl told me that she had once boasted the Spirit could never catch her, and that very night she was "cut down." In another instance, she was planning to sneak out to the cinema after church, but the Spirit threw her down, tore her dress, and messed her hair so badly that she could not. The Spirit punishes people who have been disobedient to Yeboa; one night it "cut" a ruffian who had been standing just outside the shed mocking. In the first years of Eden, people were occasionally injured, but realizing that the police would be less lenient with him now than they apparently were with the apostle Peter in the case of Ananias and Sapphira (Acts 5:1-11), Yeboa has carefully trained his nurses how to protect people under the Spirit's influence from themselves without interfering with their movements. Regular church members, although they still find it wonderful, are used to the Spirit's power. It does not frighten them unless they have been especially wicked.

Since Yeboa cannot always be with all the people who depend on his protection, he blesses handkerchiefs, water, Bibles, perfumed water, medicines, and olive oil for people to take home with them. Most church members have small altars at home, and until recently this was considered an essential part of Eden's piety. Some people, especially new members, treat these holy objects as talismans to protect themselves and heal others. Native medicine men *(odunsini)* also give people perfumed water, and several Edenians told me they use it "because the devil doesn't like its smell." The priests at pagan shrines mix potions to be used in their patients' bath water, and many people expect the same sort of protection from spiritual church leaders. Yeboa laments this weakness in faith, but says that if he gives them no "point of contact with the power source, they will run to a fetish as soon as they have a terrible dream. They must be given spiritual milk; later they will learn that Christ is always with them."

A few Edenians have matured to that point. Those who come forward for prayers in church tend to be newcomers. At least in theory, the more mature members get sick less often. Even if they are ill, they tend to pray for themselves rather than depend on Yeboa. The people who have followed Yeboa for a long time are not afraid to pray for others, and although their results are not as spectacular as Yeboa's, people are healed.

Spiritual Development

Eden Revival Church exercises spiritual power, not only

68

by effective prayer but also through supernatural knowledge. The process by which a Christian moves from "a mere intellectual knowledge" to "an experience of the power of Jesus" in dreams and visions is called "spiritual development." "Spiritual development" is considered "the only means by which we can give permanence to our salvation."

Edenians, like most other Ghanaians, think of their dreams as messages from the spirit world. According to Yeboa, "The subconscious is on the supernatural plane." The developing Christian may pass from dreams to hearing voices, then to waking visions, and finally to the point where visions can be voluntarily induced:

> Participation in divine things becomes more real . . . as the divinely invisible plane acts directly upon the Christian.[6]

Careful diet and fasting are the tools Edenians use to open the door to the spirit world. According to Yeboa, "Food is a burden," so he never eats much and is careful about what he does eat. He read that Adam did not kill animals for food (Gen. 1:29) and that Daniel became wise and strong by shunning meat and rich food (Dan. 1:12). He believes that since meat and eggs become especially foul in time, they must not be good for the body. Animals seem to him to feel pain more than men; he says a goat struck by a car will writhe more than a man unless the man has eaten a lot of meat. If someone is hot-tempered or suffers great pain, Yeboa teaches that a vegetarian diet will calm him.

Yeboa never eats meat, eggs, fufu, pepper, rich foods, alcohol, or stimulants, and he has learned from experience that this makes him more vital and alert. He drinks a lot of water, and there seems to him to be a special affinity between the Spirit and water; in this regard he cites the Creation account, "The Spirit of God was moving over the face of the waters" (Gen. 1:2). A few Edenians follow Yeboa's example, at least to the extent of shunning rich foods and alcohol.

A greater number of Edenians practice occasional fasts. Yeboa has lived on water alone for 40 days three times, once preceding a 40-day fast by 20 days of eating nothing but oranges.

The other pastors have all done marathon fasts too. Church members are supposed to go without food one day a week, and most regular members do, in fact, observe one- to three-day fasts once in a while.

It is said that fasting leads to meekness, dependence on God, and obedience. It sharpens the mind and cures many diseases. Not least important, if someone fasts for a long time, the Spirit may grant special dreams and visions. Yeboa once said:

> Fasting is the greatest gift in the world. I could stay in the house alone for months and have a wonderful time. Other people go to cinemas, but I see better things than that right here. Oh, it's wonderful! You start jumping, and hearing things, and speaking in strange tongues. But then you've got to control yourself, or people around will think you are mad.

In using fasting as an aid to visions, Yeboa is following several Biblical examples: Moses (Ex. 34:28), Elijah (1 Kings 19:8), and Jesus. (Matt. 4:2)

The Spirit is thought to use men who are especially "developed" to guide other people and the church. Most Edenians refuse to go to assistant pastors for counsel because they believe that Yeboa is better able to tell them secrets about themselves. In the past Yeboa would sometimes even stop a stranger on the street to advise him on the basis of some special revelation, and several of Eden's most faithful members first became connected with Yeboa in this way. Many others were convinced of Yeboa's power when he was able to divine some hidden incident in their past, just as the Samaritan woman came to think Jesus might be the Messiah when He told her about her five husbands. (John 4:16-19)

Major church decisions, especially in the early years, were always confirmed by visions. Week by week the Spirit supposedly leads Eden's pastors in preaching. None of them write their sermons in advance; they study in preparation, but think that written notes would show a lack of faith. Opong, pastor of Kumasi's Eden, always fasts the day of a sermon. He prays on his bed, and if he falls asleep he often dreams of himself preach-

70

ing. After checking the dream sermon against the Bible, he gives the inspired message in church.

It is believed that visions often predict the future. One university graduate told me with amazement about a dream in which he saw his name with his degree letters written after it several months before he finally passed. A dream or vision of this sort does not seem to be ever fully understood until after the fact. For example, months before the 1969 election Yeboa had a vision in which Dr. Busia was hoisted on other men's shoulders in a victory celebration, but Busia seemed to beckon to a stranger standing to one side. Until after Busia's landslide victory, Yeboa suspected this might mean that Busia would be elected, but without a convincing majority. He did not announce the vision publicly until the election results had been announced, and then he did not mention the mysterious stranger he had seen.

Yeboa's supernatural knowledge is thought to include clairvoyance and clairaudience. This is a very effective belief in helping Edenians lead moral lives, because they believe whatever they do Yeboa will know. Yeboa surprised me several times by telling me what I had been doing while we were apart, but in two instances I was able to trace his knowledge back to a member of the church acting as informant.

Visions sometimes are said to reveal secrets from the spirit world. Pastor Buabeng is fascinated with apocryphal literature about angels and evil powers, which he justifies on the basis of Jesus' words:

> I have yet many things to say to you, but you cannot bear them now. When the Spirit of truth comes, He will guide you into all the truth (John 16:12-13).

Yeboa has, in the past, counseled people on the basis of their "past lives." The doctrine of reincarnation is widely known and believed among Akans, but Yeboa rationalizes its use in a Christian church as a special revelation by the Spirit to him.

Ghanaians tend to be insistently curious about particular happenings. They may know, for example, that malaria is caused by mosquito bites. Not everybody bitten by a mosquito, however, gets the disease, and Edenians want to know why a particular person gets malaria at a particular time. If they ask, "Why am *I* sick?" no medical generalization will satisfy them. Spiritual knowledge, unlike science, is almost always personal. It most often answers questions like: What should the preacher say to his people *this* Sunday? Will *I* succeed in business? What are *my* strengths and weaknesses?

When Yeboa "reads" people, he usually speaks in terms of astrology or perhaps palmistry. He believes that people born in different months have distinctive characteristics, and he keeps a list of people and their birth dates as part of his own religious research. In our times, he says, most men study outer space, but astrological charts are a remnant of the findings of ancient men who studied man, God, and nature.

An astrologer calculates a man's character by the time and place of his birth, but Yeboa says this may be inaccurate, since astrological calculations seldom include winds, earthquakes, and other disturbances. Yeboa claims to achieve better results by "reading men spiritually," depending upon prayer. The better he knows a man, he admits, the more accurate his reading. These readings are almost invariably delivered, however, in terms of "cosmic forces" and "astral influences." It is argued that God inspired the Wise Men through a star (Matt. 2:2), and Jacob's prophesies (Gen. 49) are coupled with the 12 tribes of men in Revelation (Rev. 7:4-8) to justify grouping people into 12 groups according to birth.

Supernatural knowledge has become less important as Eden has matured. Some people say it is because Yeboa has been too busy with the schools to fast and pray. In fact, Yeboa rarely fasts now. He says it is because prophets who depend too much on visions finally lose touch with everyday reality and may even become insane.

In 1968 Yeboa crashed his automobile because of a horrible vision. He was driving when he suddenly saw fetish priests lining the road, and he recalls something beating on his head. His arms became stiff, so he had to steer with his chest, but he did not tell the others in the car. He thought, "Why did I come into the world anyway?" He saw himself running up a hill; this double of himself looked back at him and told him to crash the car. He swerved into a ditch. Several people were badly hurt, and although his finger bone was protruding from the flesh, as soon as he realized what he had done, he began praying for everybody, "O God, I would rather die myself than have anybody else in the car die!" Everyone recovered, but Yeboa remembers the incident as "the worst experience of my life."

Later he saw a vision of his body; it was transparent, so that he could see inside it. He said to himself, "You had better be careful. Moses only fasted 40 days twice, and you've already done it three times. Quit trying to be an angel." Now instead of always seeking visions, he prays for wisdom.

He resents being used as a soothsayer, and complains that people who are accustomed to pagan shrines or other spiritual churches are so eager for him to tell them secrets about themselves. This is the most dangerous thing in the church, he once said, because even more than healing, it can make men dependent on the preacher instead of God.

One of the girls who has been in Eden since it was a small prayer group in Nsawam wrote the following hymn; it is seldom sung in church, but it looks forward to the day when the spiritual churches will have succeeded and many Ghanaians other than special holy men will have spiritual power:

> *Kama me kama me nni ho bio*
> *Kama me kama me nni ho bio*
> *Aoh daano kama me nni ho bio*
> *daa odiyofo nni ho bio da no*
> *nsɛm nyinaa bɛda adi*
>
> "Plead for me" will be no more,
> "Plead for me" will be no more,
> On that day "Plead for me" will be no more.
> On that day no prophet,
> On that day all secret things will be exposed.

CHAPTER FIVE

Eden's Worship

There are hundreds of diverse spiritual churches in Ghana. They vary in size from a few children parading behind a neighborhood prophet to the tens of thousands listed as regular members of the Divine Healer's Church, and they vary in ritual from sects which sacrifice chickens for various spirits to a church as orthodox as Eden.

Virtually all spiritual church worship is embellished with manifestations of spiritual power: trances, faith healing, reported visions. Late night music — drumming, clapping, singing hour after hour — is also nearly universal. Most spiritual churches borrow hymns from the Methodists and Presbyterians, rituals from the Roman Catholics and Anglicans. All the churches draw upon a growing collection of lively spiritual folk hymns that circulate freely among them.

In the centuries of war, mass migrations, and social upheaval which preceded colonialism in west Africa, Ghana accumulated an immense collection of divergent rites. This pool of African practices has been further enriched and polluted by Christian missions, secret societies, texts on home remedies, occult tracts, visiting yogis, astrology columns in the newspapers, manufactured magical paraphernalia, and the jargon of modern psychology. Each prophet selects a distinctive mixture from this heritage and, if he is clever, adds a few innovations to set himself apart.

Eden's worship is not typical of spiritual churches. Yeboa is extraordinarily innovative in planning Eden's worship. He has borrowed heavily from American Pentecostal churches and is self-consciously trying to earn the respect of orthodox churches. Eden is larger, and its services more formally organized, more complicated, and more flamboyant than those of most spiritual churches. Perhaps a dozen women and a few semiliterate men would be more typical, but those few men would probably change their little flock into an Eden Revival Church if they could. Eden's worship is a model for many lesser prophets in the spiritual church movement.

Liturgy

Eden services are noisy, joyful, almost carefree. The worship is a group activity, and little time is given for staid meditation or silent prayer. The continuous singing and hand-clapping makes introspection almost impossible. People might come just to have a good time; the music is better than at many night-clubs, Yeboa's show is more exciting than the cinema, and it is all free. But the celebration, however exuberant, is deeply religious.

Eden's worship usually follows one of two patterns. On Wednesday nights the emphasis is on healing; the sermon only gets the people in the mood for miracles, and prayers for all sorts of ailments last late into the night. The Sunday service is shorter and less emotional; teaching is the main purpose, and the short healing rite that precedes the sermon is only to relieve pains that might distract people as the preacher expounds God's laws.

Yeboa alters each service as the Spirit leads him. He invents enough different rituals so that the congregation never knows quite what to expect. He calls various groups forward for prayers: the sick, or perhaps just those ailing from the waist up, pregnant women, barren women, new members, people troubled by dreams, those whom he has counseled privately, individuals about whom he has seen visions, those who have contributed to the church regularly, all the men or all the women, and so on. There are a host of Sunday services made special by prayers for the nation, a congregational fast, or perhaps a society anniversary to which branch congregations are invited.

75

On a typical Sunday morning by nine o'clock most of the Women's Fellowship, dressed in zebra-striped skirts and white blouses, have already gathered in Eden's shed at Kokomlemle. They sing and clap as more people gradually arrive, take off their shoes, and sit down. A few ladies in the Workers' Association sit near the front, distinctive in yellow skirts and lacy, white blouses. The Singing Stars, dressed in blue, take their place nearby. Children sit together in the right-hand row of benches, men in the right-center row, and women throughout the rest of the church.

When the band joins in a little before ten o'clock, the church is almost full. Three saxophones, two brass, and a five-man percussion section begin to accompany the singing with "High Life," a type of popular music in Ghana. The big shed begins to reverberate, and the Women's Fellowship dances out onto the tiled space before the altar. They circle twice, their steps ranging from a simple walk through a fairly complicated shuffle. When they return to their seats, about 30 other ladies dance out to take their place. Some swing their handkerchiefs in happy circles, and there are pantomime motions for a few of the hymns.

About half past ten the choir, robed in gold and black but barefoot, processes. The assistant pastor makes some announcements, offers a prayer and the Lord's Prayer, and reads a psalm. Most of the spoken parts of the service are first given in English, then repeated in Twi with a simultaneous translation into Ga. These preliminaries take half an hour because he seldom speaks long without calling for more singing. Meanwhile, Brother Yeboa himself enters and takes his seat near the altar.

The assistant pastor explains the purpose of healing at this service:

> If you have a pain in your back or your stomach is aching, it will be difficult for you to listen to the Word. You will be thinking of your physical troubles instead of the message. So I would like all those with illnesses to come forward now.

About 60 people with various troubles form several lines facing the altar, bow their heads, and close their eyes. The band starts playing, and the whole congregation claps in rhythm.

Finally, Yeboa begins to move. At first he walks across the front of the church, throwing handfuls of water out across the crowd of sick. A number of people gasp and jump, and a few lose control of themselves more completely. He begins singling out certain people for special blessings. Sometimes he asks a few questions about the problem and massages the ailing area. He almost always sprinkles his patient with water, presses a hand against his forehead, and wrestles out a prayer. Most patients are obviously moved by the Spirit—fainting, jumping wildly, or falling and flailing on the floor. Soon there are five or six people on the ground, rolling back and forth, quivering, and kicking spasmodically. An attendant moves up and down the rows praying for each supplicant in turn, but Yeboa works as the Spirit moves him. He grapples with one or two illnesses, then retires to the altar to wipe his hands, then is suddenly out among the people again.

After each supplicant has received some individual attention, the assistant pastor asks those who have been healed to come forward:

> We will sing one more song, and I want you to test it. Come up here if it is better. But even Jesus had to try twice to heal the blind boy, and if you are still sick, it does not mean that God has no love for you. If you are not better, do not come forward.

Nearly half the people step toward the front, and the assistant says a last prayer for each of them.

Yeboa continues moving among those not yet healed. He steps out to encourage the congregation to sing louder, then turns and touches the shoulder of an old woman already jumping up and down. She begins to dance in dizzying circles, so several attendants form a ring around her in case she should slip. Yeboa struggles with some people's illnesses two or three times. A few return to their seats disappointed, but most finally notice some improvement and go forward for a final prayer.

After the healing the choir sings a few hymns, swaying together to the rhythm. They use European melodies with Twi lyrics. The Singing Stars stand and sing one hymn set to indigenous music.

Then everyone sings and dances. It is already past noon, but nobody is ready to go home. Several women are thrown from their seats by the Spirit. Lines of people dance before the altar and through the aisles. Even the men, usually more staid, join the celebration and dance one great circle around the congregation.

When the singing stops, Reverend Yeboa begins to preach. He is a master orator, especially in Twi:

> Praise Him! [The people answer "Alleluia!"] Since the inception of the world, since the very beginning, God has promised, no matter where men go, to give them His Spirit power! The devil is everywhere. His laws are all around us. There are idols all over Ghana, altars in many homes. But God promises Spirit power! Praise Him! ["Alleluia!"]

Yeboa is all energy — moving, fidgeting, twisting, his voice now booming, now pleading. Now he has abandoned the lectern and hovers over the first row of the congregation:

> You can have that Spirit power when you make one decision, when you decide to follow Christ's laws, and no other laws — Christ's laws first, and the nation's laws second. Some people will tell you there are other laws, but they are here (waving the Bible). Now the devil is ready to destroy you — by juju, by witchcraft, by dangerous drugs, by getting you put behind prison bars. He is ready to vex you, the moderner. So I want you to hear what happened to Peter.

The headmaster of the secondary school begins to read from the 12th chapter of Acts:

> At the same time Herod, the king, stretched forth his hands to afflict some of the church. He killed James . . . [Yeboa exclaims, "He killed James!"] . . . the brother of John with the sword. And, seeing also that it pleased the Jews, he proceeded to take up Peter also.

78

Before the headmaster reads another sentence from the Bible, Yeboa interprets:

> When you follow Jesus, He will give you the key to resurrection, to eternal life! You can obey the laws, even if the devil kills you. God allowed James to be killed, so that we would know that even if you die, you will go on living with Christ.

The dialog between Scripture and preacher continues, occasionally interrupted by more singing. Yeboa explains difficult passages, repeats others for emphasis, applies the lesson to Ghanaian life, and sometimes rambles off into apparently unrelated topics. He preaches for about 10 minutes in English, then after a round of hymns delivers the message again in Twi, and a woman nearby translates it into Ga.

When Yeboa finally announces the offertory, it is almost one o'clock. The congregation sings, and those with regular pledges line up, walk forward to the collection plate, and drop in a *cedi* (equivalent to an American dollar) or more each. Yeboa dons a black robe and prays for each of these benefactors individually. Most of them simply relax into the attendants' arms; one or two kick spasmodically for a few seconds after he handles them. Yeboa then calls for unpledged gifts, and everyone in the church dances forward in turn. Most people can only afford to give small coins, but the women compete with the men to see which group will give more, and some are moved to come forward more than once with contributions. They love to dance and evidently love to give, because it is at this point in the service that everyone seems most jubilant. Yeboa appeals for money several times, and even though the offertory dancing continues for over an hour, smiles are broad and genuine to the end.

Nearly every Sunday there is some sort of special ceremony near the end of the service. Sometimes those with membership cards bring them to the altar. Occasionally Yeboa publicly reveals a vision he has had about somebody in the congregation. This Sunday he prays for each of the people visiting Eden for the first time and invites them to join the church. Then Yeboa offers a final prayer and leaves as the congregation sings a slow, quiet benediction.

Symbolism

The symbolism at an Eden service is polyglot and powerful. Outside are big "Eden" billboards, and another sign labels the vacant lot next to the shed the "Garden of Eden." The name "Eden" is particularly alluring to west African Christians because precolonial religion taught about God primarily as the Creator. According to traditional religious stories, men offended God soon after the Creation, and God left the world; since God is no longer involved in earthly affairs, petitions are to be addressed to lesser spirits. "Eden Revival" signals a communion with God as intimate as that of the first men.

An Eden service is a public drama in which various people act out their own particular roles. Yeboa ritually demonstrates God's conquest over sin and sickness. The nurses tenderly care for those who have lost control of themselves, allowing those "caught by the Spirit" to bang against their bodies rather than fall on the floor or against a chair. The choir and band, mostly young and educated, offer their musical proficiency to God. The less educated Singing Stars share indigenous songs. And the members of the Women's Fellowship, mostly illiterate, enthusiastically lead the congregation in singing the simple spiritual hymns. Public worship is also a time for financial celebration, and especially people in the Workers' Association, among the wealthiest in the church, dance forward again and again dropping bills into the collection plate.

The church's several functions are also visually apparent. The organ and choir robes, the uniforms of the Singing Stars and Women's Fellowship, the altar and lectern could be found in any Presbyterian or Methodist church in Ghana. The people are, however, less formally dressed, and the band reminds one, particularly in the night lights of a Wednesday service, of an entertainment spot. The ushers and attendants are dressed exactly like orderlies and nurses in a medical hospital.

Above the church altar is a large, lighted cross in red and white with a sacred heart and a picture of Jesus — compassionate almost to the point of femininity — at its center and "Eden" spelled out at the top. The altar is flanked by two painted murals:

80

on the left an angel slaying the devil and, on the right, the last judgment. The one on the left symbolizes power, the one on the right represents law. In both murals Christ and His angels are pictured as white men; the devil is painted black.

No one wears shoes in church, partly so that people will be comfortable and pay attention, partly as a mark of respect. One man joining the church listed this as a major reason. He said he always takes off his shoes to enter his own or his father's room, but orthodox Christians tramp all sorts of dirt into the house of God. He cited the command to Moses, "Take off your shoes, for you are standing on holy ground." (Ex. 3:5)

Eden has only recently become sufficiently established to begin performing rites of passage and celebrating sacraments. Ntiforo and Rutishauser, in their description of the typical spiritual church, write:

> The last step in the development towards a regular Church is when the group starts to administer sacraments. It is interesting to note that leaders are on the whole very reluctant to take this last step, often resisting considerable pressure from their followers.[1]

The example of Eden Revival Church supports this observation.

Yeboa conducted his first church wedding only recently. Almost all Ghanaian marriages are settled by the two families without a church wedding anyway. He has conducted several funerals. The church band and several lorries of Edenians go to the bereaved family's home for hymn singing, and then after a few hours the body is taken to the grave. ˙

During 1969 Eden began to baptize. Virtually everyone who joins the church is now rebaptized. In June nearly the entire Accra congregation was "thoroughly immersed in spiritualism" in a river outside the city. A few months later 50 more were baptized there, those who had been away before and new members. In late 1969 Yeboa made trips to Begoro and Nkawkaw to baptize the congregations there.

At a baptism ceremony those who are to be baptized gather quietly at the bank of the river, all dressed in white. There is little conversation. When Yeboa arrives, they sing some spiritual songs. He preaches to them, perhaps telling them that baptism is the water of life, the answer to sin and resultant sickness and death: "We are buried with Christ by baptism into death, so that with Him we will rise to eternal life" (Rom. 6:4). Yeboa blesses everyone before they go into the water, but following the example of Paul (1 Cor. 1:14), he lets junior pastors conduct the actual baptism, lest someone say he received special power by Yeboa's baptism. As they are helped out of the river, many people are "caught by the Spirit," and unless they are held carefully, one or two may run wildly into the bush for hours. Spiritual songs are sung throughout the service, and they close, usually a little before dark, with a quiet prayer.

The Lord's Supper is celebrated once a year. Yeboa argues that it was originally part of Passover, so that weekly Communion is counter to God's ordinance. Also, since "familiarity breeds contempt," it is thought better to give the Lord's Supper infrequently and make it an impressive occasion.

Hymns

The constant in all Eden worship is the singing. Eden's hymns are short and lively; one easily remembered verse is repeated again and again. They are usually cast in general terms, conveying basic attitudes rather than explicating doctrines, and are appropriate for all sorts of situations. Eden's commercial records are appreciated throughout Ghana, and I have heard strangers, as well as regular church members, humming the familiar tunes as they go about their business.

When Edenians socialize together, they may entertain themselves with Eden hymns. As people gather during the hour or so before a service, the Women's Fellowship leads them in song. An Eden preacher never begins without the inspiration of a song, and he calls for hymn breaks again and again throughout the sermon. Spirited singing is a crucial part of the healing process. If a hymn begins to drag during the long healing service, Brother Yeboa will encourage the congregation to sing with more enthusiasm, because he knows he needs their help to cure his patients. Eden's music is the staple of their worship, and especially the women seem to be able to pass hour after hour blissfully singing spiritual hymns.

The sudden appearance of hundreds of little hymns, many of them delightful, is a notable explosion of creativity. Eden Revival Church has borrowed about half of its most commonly used songs from other spiritual churches. Since many Edenians attend other churches too, they bring new songs back to Eden and teach them, first to the Women's Fellowship, and then to the whole church. The other half of Eden's songs were written by members of the church; not many spiritual churches could claim such a high proportion of original songs. A relatively small number of members write most of Eden's songs, but they receive little recognition for their creativity. They say the lyrics and tunes seem to come by inspiration.

Most of the spiritual church songs are variations on one theme: God is victorious. Less than a fourth of them make any mention of human responsibility. Even though many worshipers have specific and urgent needs, only a few are petitions. Most of them are phrased in faith, praising and thanking God as if He had already intervened to solve all problems. A typical spiritual church song is:

> *Tumi nyinaa ɛyɛ wode,*
> *Tumi nyinaa ɛyɛ wode,*
> *Wona wo bo soro asase,*
> *Oo tumi nyinaa ɛyɛ wode.*
>
> All power is Yours,
> All power is Yours,
> You created heaven and earth,
> O, all power is Yours.

Doubt, struggle, and self-examination have little place in the lyrics of these folk psalms; they are preoccupied with the celebration of God's life-giving power.[2]

The new spiritual songs of Africa, together with the spirituals of Afro-Americans, constitute an extraordinarily impressive library of Christian hymns, most of them expressive of the irrepressible faith in God which is so characteristic of Afro-Christianity. The delightful worship of Eden, similar to indigenous church services in most parts of Africa and among many Afro-Americans, is part of one of the most vital, enjoyable liturgical traditions in Christendom.

CHAPTER SIX

The Eden Community

How can members of a big church like Eden still talk about it as if it were a family? What is the relationship of Eden's schools to the church? What is Yeboa's position within the church? Why is the church made up predominantly of women? These are the major questions to be considered in this chapter. The chapter is about the social structure of Eden Revival Church, about groupings within the church, and about the distinctive ways in which the members of Eden interact.

Societies

Most of Eden's core of regular members belong to one of the church societies. Some Eden societies have been short-lived, but during my fieldwork there were seven: Choir, Nurses, Band, Singing Stars, Women's Fellowship, Elders, and Worker's Association.

The Choir is the most time-consuming society. It is widely acknowledged to be one of the best musical groups in Ghana. Although the records they have produced for public sale have not made much money for Eden Revival Church as was intended, they became quite popular. Whenever spiritual churches gather for some sort of joint celebration, the performance of Eden's disciplined, uniformed choir is a high point of the occasion.

Although they usually sing Twi lyrics, they use European hymns and sing them in a very European style, so most of the choristers have to be at least secondary school graduates. Several Europeans and Americans have at different times been hired to further improve the Choir, and Yeboa himself usually listens to part of each rehearsal and forcefully offers his suggestions. The Choir is present at every Eden service and practices one night midweek; a faithful chorister spends at least 15 hours a week at rehearsals and services.

The Nurses are a part of the Choir, but they have added responsibilities. They act as ushers during services, keeping order and carrying out errands for Yeboa. They are trained to help during healing services, especially to protect the people who are "caught" by the Spirit from hurting themselves. They are usually among the people who have been faithful to Eden for the longest time.

Musical instruments must be imported to Ghana and are very expensive. The Eden Band's collection is exceptional. The Choir seldom performs or rehearses without the Band, but the Band is not as expert because they have not received as much special training.

The Singing Stars perform indigenous Twi songs. They are generally less educated than Choir and Band members, and their songs sound much more African. Mr. Antwi, the director, writes many of these songs himself. The Singing Stars perform some Sundays, but not as regularly as the Choir. The Singing Stars usually meet for rehearsals midweek, but attendance at these rehearsals is sometimes a problem.

The Women's Fellowship is responsible for leading congregational singing. Most of the members are middle-aged, illiterate ladies. They are always at church before anyone else, and they frequently stay after the service to learn new songs. Their enthusiasm for singing and dancing during the services is an inspiration to everybody else.

The Elders are supposed to advise Yeboa and help lead the church. This is a precarious role, and several times the Elders have virtually ceased to exist temporarily because of a quarrel between one or two of them and Yeboa. They meet on call, usually once a month.

The Workers' Association is supposed to raise money and carry out special projects for the church. They are the newest of the societies, but have been torn almost since they began by quarrels within the group. The Workers' Association includes some of the wealthiest members of Eden, but the organization is weak, and they meet very irregularly. Several of the women in the group, however, usually wear their Workers' Association uniforms to church.

After someone has been healed by Eden, Yeboa assigns them to a society as soon as possible. The societies provide especially close fellowship. Eden Revival Church can be a close community despite its size because of the societies. As a young man who was in the process of joining Eden said:

> Edenians love their church. They treat each other like blood relatives. There are so many Catholics, you don't even know who they are. But Edenians greet each other on the street like brothers and sisters.

People get to know each other in the societies, and genuine friendships grow. Often society members visit each other during the week, not to talk about church business, but simply because they have become friends. If a faithful member is in critical need, his society provides spiritual and perhaps some kind of material support.

Members of Eden are relatively estranged from their natural families. The church is centered in Accra, and all its branches are in major towns. Many of its members are the exceptional people who dared to leave their rural homes, perhaps as children with their parents, to join the materialistic bustle, the confusion of tribes and tongues, the monumental effort to imitate the West that characterizes urban Ghana. Most of them resist traditional kinship obligations. A few of the most loyal were born of parents from two tribes with different kinship systems so that they are effectively without an extended family. For such people it is very important that Eden Revival Church be as intensely communal as is possible in a modern city.

Eden's closeness accounts for much of the church's healing and reforming power. Joining a society may give someone who has been healed enough confidence to keep himself free of a spiritual malady. Society membership is often the final cure for alcoholism. In the societies morality is not a private matter; it is something shared. The societies, like little urban villages, reinforce morality by social pressure and counteract the demoralizing effects of urbanization.

Schools

The mission churches, particularly the Methodists and Presbyterians, have always invested heavily in schools in Ghana. After 1966 Eden Revival Church began organizing its own schools. Eden was the second spiritual church to have schools of its own, following by 20 years the lead of Prophet Wovenu's Apostolic Revelation Society.

Yeboa says he felt a real need for Christian, disciplined education in Ghana. The government schools were producing students without morals, and Yeboa thought Eden's schools could inculcate the sense of responsibility and readiness to obey he thinks are lacking in modern Ghanaian youth. Also, since primary schools are often of low quality and government secondary schools don't have room for everybody who wants to attend, private schools can be good business in Ghana. Eden Revival Church needed another source of funds if it were to expand.

Eden now operates a good-quality primary school for 150 students. Most of the 300 students in Eden Secondary School failed to get into government schools. In addition, Eden maintains a business school for 50 students. To date these schools have not been profitable. School fees have been invested in school improvements. The schools operate on low budgets, depending heavily on the dedication of a number of church members who work in the schools.

Not many of the faculty and students are affiliated with Eden Revival Church. Students are required to attend morning devotions daily and Sunday evening services, but these exercises are received with little enthusiasm. Some faculty and students are Moslems, some pagan, some members of other churches, and some are skeptical about all religion.

Leader and People

Traditional Akan society is generally authoritarian. A father cares for the people in his household, but wives and children are expected to be humble and subservient, and he might even possibly beat them if they disobey. The chief is like a father to his people, their representative before the ancestors, and owner of all the land. In religious life, a fetish priest exercises a benevolent dictatorship over his counselors, junior priests and priestesses, and others in his house.

Yeboa is like a father, chief, and priest to church members. They come to him for advice, and he helps them make decisions and, if necessary, gives them money or helps them find a job. If, on the other hand, they are wayward, he punishes them with the Spirit and on rare occasions even beats them physically. He sometimes plays the role of a parent when girls in the church get married; he chooses men for them and charges them with their responsibilities as husbands.

Yeboa's leadership is nearly absolute. He listens to the advice of those around him, but he makes final decisions alone. Society leaders relay his orders to the people. The headmasters of the schools carry out his policies. Yeboa himself is extraordinarily efficient and subleaders rarely satisfy him, so he ends up doing almost everything himself—coaching the choir, choosing books for the schools, supervising workmen constructing a volleyball court, and so on—but he complains that the work is too much for one man.

The branch churches, simply because distance keeps Yeboa away, have some independence. Outstation congregations learn to trust their own pastors. The local elders control church finances. Pastors and elders together make day-to-day decisions on their own. But far-reaching decisions are made by Yeboa, and all the branches are miniature copies of Eden in

Accra. Most of the pastors are Yeboa's relatives, he moves them about or dismisses them all with complete freedom, and, as one of them said, "I will obey Teacher absolutely, unless I judge him to be in opposition to the Bible."

Yeboa built Eden almost singlehandedly, and he alone controls finances. Until recently no account of funds was made. Now he has shown a record of income and expenses to church elders and to me, but anyone else who contributes to Eden simply has to trust Yeboa. This has been a major source of strife in the church, especially since Yeboa dresses in the latest fashions, lives in a fine house, and drives a luxury car. His apparent prosperity is in one regard an asset for the church, because it inspires faith in those who come praying for material blessings. Conspicuous consumption can also cause envy, however.

In fact, all the offerings are used for maintaining the church and evangelism—no mean tasks without support from abroad. Yeboa buys nothing for himself; his clothes are all gifts, his house belongs to another man. His life is completely given over to Eden. He is not using the church to build up private wealth. And since he is adventurous, instead of putting money in the bank, he always launches a new idea.

It is true, however, that control over Eden's assets adds to Yeboa's power. He told me:

> Someday, after Eden's foundations are laid, elders will handle the money and employ pastors as professional men. But then some of the power will be gone, because the pastors will always be afraid.

About 25 church members are employed in the church, which means, in effect, they work for Yeboa. Many of them also live in one of the several houses he maintains. Some of them "consider the work their own" and at times refuse money he offers them. He, in turn, is liberal in giving to these faithful few. Even those employees in the church with regular salaries seem to be paid less than they could receive elsewhere, but Yeboa supplements their income with gifts. The financial relationships here are personal and familial rather than official and bureaucratic.

If people who come to Yeboa for prayers also need money, as a Christian pastor he often finds it difficult to refuse. Money is scarce in Ghana, and men who borrow may assume the role of client. If Yeboa makes gifts or loans to people in need, they are naturally eager to show him gratitude.

As a result of the combination of spiritual and financial power in Yeboa, people fear him. They refer to him as "Teacher," "that man," or "the big man," but almost never call him by name. I was told that the only time someone in Eden tried to lay hands on Yeboa to pray for him, the Spirit threw her across the room and onto the floor. Harsh words from him are genuinely frightening, even to men as well-established as himself. The girls closest to him begin to cry if he scolds them at all. Many young men are afraid even to come into his house.

Yeboa says he keeps himself "somehow separate" to maintain his leadership. He has cut virtually all ties with his home, and never goes out with friends. He does not socialize freely with anyone: "Otherwise the power in Eden would crumble." If any of Eden's original power is eroding, as many people say, he thinks it is because Edenians are more familiar with him now: "A prophet is without honor in his own country." (Luke 4:24)

Yeboa owns more property, is reputed to have effected more cures, is more forceful, and commands a larger following than almost any other churchman in Ghana. He can therefore also afford to be one of the most authoritarian, least compromising church leaders in Ghana.

Women and Men

Women predominate in most churches everywhere, but particularly in Ghanaian spiritual churches. Yeboa gave several reasons why in Eden Revival Church the woman are more faithful than the men:

> Women are born to believe. Men don't believe much in unseen things. Besides, women have more problems. They hear there is power here, so they may get help. Also, in Africa the women

are born to serve. Here a woman will carry a heavy load, have a baby on her back, and be chopping wood. They serve at home, so they serve in the church.

The third factor Yeboa mentioned, female subservience, is especially important in keeping them in spiritual churches. There are usually twice as many women in Eden services as men, and more than twice as many contributors; almost all the employees of Eden, except for Yeboa's relatives and a few exceptionally selfless workers, are women — mostly young girls — because they are willing to obey.

Yeboa is a handsome 31-year-old man, and his charisma is naturally more effective with women. Because of the extensive physical contact he uses in praying for people, this sexual attraction could be explosive:

This is our problem. The women have built this church from the beginning. Some come because they are frustrated, some because they love us. But as a pastor we ought to be able to handle all of these cases.

Yeboa is exceptional among Ghanaian men, especially among spiritual church leaders, in rigorously maintaining his chastity. He plans to take a wife eventually, but not a member of the church; he is sure that marriage to one of the girls in Eden would be terribly divisive.

I counted 389 attending one Wednesday night service: 206 women, 92 children, and 91 men. Most of the children came with their mothers, although a few from the neighborhood were by themselves. Thirty-eight of the men stood outside the big shed looking in! Some were young rowdies who like Eden's music but want to be able to move around and talk if they like. Most, however, watched intently throughout the service. They may have been curious, almost believing, but not ready to identify themselves with the church.

Most of the men who are heavily involved in Eden's day-to-day work sometimes chafe under Yeboa's yoke. Elders have quit one after another. I know of at least two pastors who tried unsuccessfully to break with Yeboa and take part of his membership into their own churches before I arrived. During the four months I stayed in Yeboa's house one pastor was dismissed for immorality, one pastor in training left in anger, and two other young men who were considering being Eden pastors left after a few days. Another pastor was banned from Eden's pulpit for secretly starting an evangelistic association of his own. One faithful Eden pastor was trying to get aid to study in the United States. Yet another told me that he has frequently been tempted to strike out on his own and evangelize. At least five of the young men who attend Eden regularly are planning to be evangelists themselves, but want to learn from Eden first.

When men like this form their own little churches, they usually copy their parent church closely in liturgy, preaching, healing techniques, even taking a similar name for the new church. There are exceptions, but most of the men who come to Eden often and work under Yeboa submit either out of economic necessity or in order to gradually acquire similar power so they can do "some great work for God" themselves.

CHAPTER SEVEN

The People in Eden

Who comes to Eden Revival Church and why? Are they illiterate or educated, poor or rich, young or old? What sorts of problems do they most often bring to Yeboa, and are those problems really solved? How does anyone arrive at the absolute commitment to Eden Revival Church some of its most faithful members express? This last chapter of this section is about the types of individuals who together make up Eden Revival Church.

Social Characteristics

Yeboa once guessed he prays for 10,000 people during a year. Allowing for possible exaggeration and inevitable inaccuracy, undeniably thousands of people visit Eden. Most of these people make no lasting commitment to the church, and since they are so transient, it is difficult to get information about them. Some just stop to listen to the music, some are curious but uncommitted, and some who want material help leave when they get what they want or if they are disappointed. There are usually about 500 people in church at a service in Accra, 200 in Begoro, about the same number in Kumasi, and smaller congregations in Nkawkaw and Winneba. Of the 500 people who might be at an Accra service, probably 150, most of them members of societies, attend services regularly. The spiritual church movement includes a cross section of the population of Ghana. Eden Revival Church alone includes all sorts of people. Some types of people are, however, more heavily represented than others.

Yeboa has more formal education than any other spiritual church leader, and his followers are generally more educated than those of other prophets. There seem to be a large number of clerks in the church. Two professors and several others with graduate degrees are among Eden's members. Yeboa estimates that three-fourths of Eden's members can read, while only half the adult population of Accra has been to school at all.[1] The leadership, staff, and the most active members of Eden are almost all secondary school graduates, although they do not seem to read much other than the Bible and a few religious books.

Spiritual church members in Ghana are not confined to the lower classes. Several important businessmen are members of Eden, and more come to Yeboa privately for prayers. V. E. C. deGraft Johnson, a nationally known politician, identifies with Eden. Several prominent chiefs, including the chiefs of Ashanti and Akim, support Eden Revival Church.

Most Edenians, especially regular members, are Twi speakers like Yeboa. A high percentage are from his native region, Akim, and two of the branch churches are located there. Other Akan tribes, especially the Fanti, Ashanti, and Akwapim, are well-represented, and the other two branches are both in Akan territory. Accra was, before the massive migration of recent years, a Ga town, and Gas also come to Eden, but Yeboa cannot speak their language and they are underrepresented in the societies. Virtually no church members are from the poorer, less educated tribes of the Volta Region, inland, and the north. Since Christianity and colonial prosperity came together, and since spiritual churches are composed primarily of second- and third-generation Christians, the spiritual church movement has most affected the southern, better educated tribes. Remote regions of Ghana have hardly been touched by Christianity, and the spiritual churches there tend to be composed primarily of immigrants from the wealthier, more Westernized regions.

Most Edenians, of course, are urban rather than rural. All of Eden's congregations are in cities and big towns. Some people make Eden their church home immediately upon their arrival in the city, but this is not the general rule. Most church members I asked indicated they had been in the city five or more years before they joined Eden.

Regular members come to church from all over the city and nearby towns. At any service, however, there are likely to be a large number of people who live near the church, hear the music, and come to enjoy the evening.

Few old women and less old men belong to Eden. Old women are most prominent in the back rows of the church and at healing services. Eden's leadership is young, and its main appeal is to the young "moderner." Yeboa attributes this imbalance to the natural conservatism of the old and to their desire to be buried by a well-established church. The leaders of a few of the spiritual churches, for example Divine Healer's Church founded by Brother Lawson in 1952, have already become old, and their congregations are obviously more mature. Time is taking Eden in the same direction, and the church is negotiating to have separate sections of cemeteries set aside for Edenians as is done for members of the orthodox churches.

The typical regular Edenian is a second- or third-generation

94

Christian, reared as a Presbyterian or, less likely, as a Methodist. He still attends his former church too, although this is less common in Eden than it used to be. Transient members range from staunch members of orthodox churches to old women who are used to pagan shrines, but in general they seem to be less faithful members of orthodox churches than regular Edenians are or have been.

Varieties of Needs

The Gospel of Discipline

Nearly everybody who comes to Eden is responding in some way to Eden's gospel of law and power. They have some special need that Eden satisfies. For many of them Eden's legalism is welcome news.

.For example, I talked with a young man from Nigeria the day he joined Eden. "Civilization is corrupting us young people," he complained. "Everybody is practicing fornication and abortion, so much so that they don't even know it is wrong." He described himself as a "fast liver" and "not the religious type." He was a Roman Catholic, but had quit going to confession because he had no will to stop certain favorite sins. Yeboa had now convinced him not to work anymore on Sunday, something he had never been able to resolve on his own, and he looked forward to a gradual reformation of his character as a member of Eden. This young man is representative of many morally confused young people in Ghanaian cities for whom discipline can be relief.

Alcoholism is a second problem in modern Ghana to which Eden's discipline can be an answer. One man about 30 years old, for example, reacted to his father's death by "drinking, smoking, and doing all sorts of terrible things." Following a friend's advice, he began attending Eden. One night Yeboa called forward all those who had been drinking and smoking. Yeboa's public prayer helped him stop drinking immediately, and he quit smoking within the week. Later he lapsed from attending Eden and started drinking heavily again. Eventually he returned to Eden, and this time joined the choir for additional support.

A third notable group of people who respond especially well to discipline are suspected witches. Yeboa says seven or eight of every ten women are witches; only about three men in a hundred are supposed to be wizards. It is believed that witches, as well as their victims, eventually suffer from their craft. Some become lame, blind, deaf, or epileptic; many go mad. The only time when witchcraft is clearly exposed is when the evil spirit drives a witch mad and she confesses her nocturnal crimes. Many women have been brought to Yeboa raving, and he has cured them through prayer, sometimes with fasting. Once the evil spirit has gone out, some of these women are afraid to leave Eden. Yeboa teaches that idolatry causes Ghana to be plagued by evil spirits, so cured witches may fear to go back to their homes where "fetishism" is practiced.

Yeboa recounted to me the story of an early miracle involving witchcraft. A girl was suffering from occasional fits, so her mother came to ask him for advice. Yeboa simply told her to ask her daughter the trouble, so she went away insulting him. But when she did ask, the girl told her that she had seen her father in a dream lying on a black dog in the middle of the road to Accra. The girl's parents had been in an automobile accident recently, and the father vaguely remembered that their driver had said the accident came about when he swerved to miss a dog in the road. The girl said the dog was really a tiger. She said that a charm her grandmother had given her as a baby made her dreams come true, and that she wanted to kill her father.

When they returned to Yeboa, he explained that he could not have accused the girl of witchcraft without risking a libel suit. He said that the girl resented obeying orders. He prayed over her again and again, but she resisted. He asked her why, and she said a voice within her told her not to obey him. He commanded the spirit to come out, and the girl became all right.

I watched another girl who had been brought to the church at Mamprobi by her mother and mother's brother. She shouted constantly in Twi, Ga, and English, sometimes saying nonsense over and over, sometimes repeating rather significant phrases like: "I don't like you," "What have I done?" or "I want to be a man!" She crawled around on the floor like an animal and once tried to tear off her clothes.

I was told by the assistant pastor who was praying for her that she was a schoolgirl. Her father had died, and although her mother's brother was obliged to provide for her, he maltreated her. Her sister and brother-in-law had gone to Britain, and some people practicing witchcraft in the house had used this girl to hurt them. She had visited them "in the spirit," appeared in their dreams at night, and they had begun to quarrel with each other so much that the man had finally sent his wife, the girl's sister back to Ghana. The witch spirit had caused madness in the girl once before, but Yeboa's prayers had cured her. When the family quit coming to church, the evil spirit had returned. This particular day Yeboa was resting, but his assistant prayed over the girl every few hours. That night she could sleep quietly, and the next day her mother was able to take her home again.

Yeboa is able to subdue rebellious witch spirits to his own iron will. His discipline is salvation to girls who have lost control of themselves. This is one reason why the girls who form the core of the church, a number of whom have been cured of witchcraft, are so absolutely obedient to Yeboa.

Healing Power

Most of the people who come to Eden are attracted by its spiritual power. The two major aspects of that power, faith healing and supernatural knowledge, are usually used together. Yeboa divines by supposedly supernatural means the hidden causes of people's problems, and then recommends the use of perfumed water, candles, or simply prayer on the basis of his spiritual diagnosis.

People bring all sorts of troubles to him. A host of minor ailments, like a "sick stomach" or a "sore neck," disappear at every Wednesday and Sunday service. Yeboa estimates that three-fourths of the people who come forward at a service are healed.

Yeboa says many women come to him for cures to gynecological ailments. Barrenness is always considered the woman's fault in Ghana, and a good number of women come to Eden seeking fertility. In one extraordinary case a woman actually seemed pregnant after Yeboa's prayers, but when the husband and Yeboa quarrelled about other matters, the apparent pregnancy collapsed. In Ghana women are also considered responsible for their children's health, and a number of women come to Eden to get help with ailing children or grandchildren.

Another common problem, especially among young men, is unemployment. Yeboa prays for the jobless, and sometimes uses his influence to find them work. One man told me how he had applied for a post in Nkrumah's Security Guard and was first rejected. Yeboa suggested that it might work for the best in the end. He finally received a letter of acceptance one day after the 1966 coup. If it had come any earlier, he probably would have been sent to prison. As further evidence of Eden's helpfulness in this area, he told me that a wealthy church member had asked the choir to choose one of its number to accept a job in his business, and the choir had decided that this man was most deserving. He explained that God helps men through other men.

Sometimes inexplicable wonders happen in Eden. I was told by several people about an accident in which a girl jumped or fell onto concrete from a second-story window but was unhurt. Yeboa prayed for her; he refused to let anyone take her to the hospital, and instead prescribed a series of baths in perfumed water. The girl never suffered more than slight bruises. Those who dislike miracles can attribute such incidents to "coincidence." To say that two things happen coincidentally means that they seem to be related but we would rather not believe they are.

Most of the major healing which I have studied involved diseases with obviously spiritual or psychological causes. For example, one of Eden's most faithful members first came to Yeboa because of a chronic ulcer. He told me he feared death from an early age. While he was in secondary school, a student acquaintance died suddenly and horribly of a bleeding ulcer. My friend was a pallbearer, and he can still vividly describe his recollection of the corpse—blood oozing from the nose and ears—and of the sight of his uncle's tombstone in the cemetery. He had horrible nightmares for weeks. He felt sure that he would get an ulcer too, and within a couple months he did. The fast life, liquor, hard work, and anxiety of university increased the trouble, until his stomach could hold nothing but milk. Finally, he began going to spiritual churches. Yeboa prescribed prayer, fasting, and Bible study; he was completely healed within three months.

Many of the people who belong to Eden first came out of fear of witchcraft. A friend of mine was plagued by horrible dreams for 15 years: Night after night he saw an old woman with a masculine body chasing him. As an adolescent he was taken to a "juju man" who healed him by rubbing powder into incisions on his wrists and temples and giving him medicine to drink. The man hinted that his mother was "eating" her boy, and my friend claims to have heard his mother and some other women come to the spiritual doctor's house in the middle of the night to get him away. They were not able to enter the house because of the strong forces inside, but when he eventually went home again, his mother did not seem to love him as she had before. He did not get sick again, but the bad dreams continued for years. Only when he joined Eden did the dreams finally stop.

At times even those spiritual powers which pagans consider helpful are troubling to Christians. A protective charm, for example, nearly destroyed a boy who plays in Eden's band. He had been hurt playing football, so his father took him to a "juju man," who healed him with leaves. He was given a talisman; he did not want to take it, but the man insisted. About a week later he began acting like a madman, and his vision became blurred and confused. When he was taken to the hospital he suddenly recovered, but as soon as they got home he went wild again. They took him to Eden and gave the talisman to Yeboa. Yeboa's prayers cured the boy, and he has been well ever since.

Susan Ofori-Ata, daughter of the paramount chief of Akim, testifies to Eden's power as it was demonstrated in a struggle with the pagan spirits in her house. As a child she participated in libations to ancestors and the worship of "small gods" with her

99

family:

> Because of our schooling it was just a custom for us. But still
> I think I was really somehow calling on my ancestors for help.

She was a regular Methodist church member, but that too was primarily a formality. She says she was basically hedonistic, and that she was going to dances, cinemas, and drinking openly.

She went to Germany for postgraduate study. After a few years there she became abnormally unhappy. She began to be haunted by ugly, decaying faces and to hear voices. The faces would chase her in visions by day, in dreams by night. She could never sleep more than a few hours at a time, and was afraid to be alone. After two months in a German psychiatric hospital she recovered, and she came back to Ghana for a summer. A few days before she was scheduled to return, the trouble came again. She was taken to Eden, and after repeated fasts she began to get stronger spiritually. She felt protected, and she saw the horrible faces less often.

Yeboa understood by supernatural means that the devil himself was haunting her because she had worshiped him with her family. She is now convinced that families with fetishes all become sickly in the long run, and she prays that her own people will realize this. If she has terrible dreams now, she thinks it is because her name is still mentioned when libation is poured at her home. Fasting and prayer help her through occasional bad days. She is now employed by Yeboa, studies the Bible passionately, is pleasant and smiling, and plans to return to Germany to continue her studies.

Case Histories of Conversion

The process through which a person is drawn into Eden Revival Church is, of course, complex. Eden's various attractions work together to convince a person to commit himself to the church. In this section two case histories are related in some detail.

The first is that of a young girl who arrived in Accra shortly before I began living in Yeboa's house. We will call her Mary. She came to the house several times a week for one month; we talked long and often. She felt guilty about all sorts of sins, but helpless to reform, and she usually complained of "feeling bad all over." I was able to watch her partial cure and reformation.

Secondly, I'll describe my own relationship to Eden Revival Church. As a student of Eden I could not have helped becoming personally involved or being myself an actor in the situation I was studying. From the beginning I tried to feel what Edenians felt and believe what they believed, rather than arrogate myself above the religion I was studying. The story of my own relationship with Yeboa is itself in retrospect an interesting case study, particularly of interest because it reveals the process through which this research was produced. The comparison between Mary and myself dramatizes Eden's inner workings, the strengths and weaknesses of the church, and the subjective dynamic involved in the spiritual church movement.

Mary, an attractive 21-year-old, had just arrived from the relatively remote region north of Kumasi when I met her. She had been her mother's firstborn, the product of a casual affair with an unknown white man. Her mother had died when Mary was 12, and she was convinced her mother's family disliked her because of her light, "bad" skin. She recalled being good, having sweet dreams, and coming to church before anyone else on Sundays as a child. After confirmation when she was 18 her life turned sour and she became immoral.

Mary's sister stayed with Yeboa for some time. She seems to have been extremely sick, and Yeboa virtually brought her back from the dead. This sister and Mary's stepmother encouraged her to go to Yeboa also. When I first met her, Mary had been in Accra nearly a month. She attended Eden because of her sister, but she said she intended to remain a Presbyterian. She liked Eden's music, but wished the services were not so long. She always sat near the back of the church so she could talk during the sermon. She said she would go to a doctor or perhaps a "magician" if she were sick, but not to a spiritual church. She wanted power like Yeboa's, but thought trance experience was a trick.

A week later Yeboa invited people who wanted to join Eden

forward for prayers, and Mary officially became a member. When Yeboa prayed for her, he hurt her neck slightly, and she appeared annoyed. The next day she applied to be a salesgirl, and Yeboa gave her a small job in the church to relieve her of her idleness in the meantime. That night he told her in my presence to "tame down and cool off." He said she ought to go back to school, but that since she was too lazy, he was praying she would get the sales job. He attributed her problem to parental laxity and treated her like a wayward child. She threatened to leave and never return, but he only laughed and called her a witch. She complained that his hand had been heavy the night before; he answered that it was the weight of the Spirit.

Mary continued to come often, but irregularly, to talk with me. She still complained of vague pains throughout her body.

About a week later Yeboa's attitude changed suddenly. The three of us had been talking, and he said, "I would pray for her, but she doesn't believe. Someday I will make the power of the Holy Spirit come over her, and she will roll and roll and roll." He put his foot on hers, grabbed her behind the back, and pushed her head down. It obviously hurt, both physically and emotionally. Yeboa was frightening, even to me; he seemed indeed to be a superhuman force incarnate. Mary had told me a few minutes before that she was feeling well, but now she said she felt ill and left.

That night she dreamed she was chased by a giant and beaten severely. She didn't sleep for the next three nights. She was especially moody and stopped visiting the house completely for several days. She said she had dreamed that Yeboa was having an affair with one of the girls in the church, and that she did not want to come to his house or be associated with such a man in any way.

That Wednesday she came to the church service, and for the first time she was caught by the Spirit. She felt something push her, her legs below the knees became very heavy, the rest of her body became very light, she fell, and the nurses had to wake her. She went home and slept for 11 hours!

She talked privately with Yeboa the next day. When I talked

with her shortly after, she was completely confused. I asked why she had come to Accra. First, she said it was in order to get a job, then to be cured, and finally because supposedly Yeboa had long ago seen a vision of her and wanted her for his wife! She explained her experience Wednesday as the Holy Spirit's work, then as a trick by Yeboa. She said that no matter what a person believes, it will work ("If I believe this flowerpot will heal me, it can heal me, but I won't be healed in Eden, because I don't believe"). She told me in detail about her dreams, accused Yeboa of promiscuity, and said the church was full of women in love with Yeboa. She claimed she did not want to be considered his girl friend too, but she also said that she looked forward to the day when she could spite him by walking in with a husband. She was afraid Yeboa would beat her someday.

During the next few days Yeboa consciously distanced himself from Mary because she acted as if she were his girl friend. Meanwhile, Mary heard gossip that some of the girls in the church were planning to beat her for being too familiar with Yeboa, and she decided to quit Eden altogether. The next night I saw her at church anyway, but she stood in the back. Yeboa mentioned to me during this period that he "saw" Mary becoming less promiscuous.

Mary's mother called and encouraged her not to believe rumors about Yeboa. Yeboa convinced her that nobody would hurt her. That night she heard a voice in her dreams telling her not to believe the stories she heard about him.

At the Sunday service, almost exactly a month after I met her, Mary listened to the sermon intently. She did not talk or even dance in church. After the service she told me that she felt as if she had become "double, like something is inside of me."

That night instead of falling asleep as usual when she tried to study the Bible at night, something jerked her back to consciousness. Later, as she lay in bed, she heard a noise in her room. She thought it might be something from God. She was too fearful to open her eyes but too excited to sleep, so she lay awake with eyes closed all night. In the morning she sat on the edge of her bed and said, "O God, what are You doing to me?"

She surprised me that Monday morning by coming at the time we had prearranged; she was not usually so reliable. She was intent that morning on correcting the damage her slander may have done. She sat down and studied English with me for an hour. She talked readily about her past, her problems and sins, and her present spiritual struggle.

She spoke with conviction about supernatural powers. She said that the devil was powerful and attributed her tendency to doze during devotions to his machinations. She told me that her brother was a witch, perhaps she was indeed a witch as Yeboa said, and that her mother's family was using witchcraft against her. She attributed her unreliability and moodiness to their craft.

She believed that God helps those who trust Him and does nothing for anybody else, so she planned to trust Him experimentally at least. She said she wanted power like Yeboa's, but that she would not get it "because I am bad." She praised Yeboa for being sympathetic, kind to everyone, and forgiving. She condemned herself as quarrelsome. It was at this time that she told me about her lonely adolescent experience, but contented herself with the thought that Yeboa really had no family either, but that, following the lyrics of a popular Eden song, he had made Jesus his "mother, father, brother, everything."

Shortly thereafter she was accepted as a salesgirl, and I saw her less during the next few months. She attended services regularly and occasionally came to the house for special prayers when she was feeling ill. Her usual attitude toward Yeboa was still exceptionally casual, but at these times she approached him in apparent terror. He would accuse her again and again, only half jokingly, of witchcraft. When he would pray over her or sometimes just move toward her, the Spirit would seize her violently. She gradually became more and more convinced of God's power and Yeboa's integrity.

In our final conversation, nearly five months after our first, Mary said her stomach pained her less often than before, that she had "calmed down" and become less argumentative. She explained the healing process simply by citing Bible miracle stories and laughed at her former ignorance of the Spirit. She identified herself strongly with Eden and defended Yeboa against his critics. Just before I left Ghana two months later, she was allowed to become one of Eden's nurses.

Although the process of healing and moral reform was still under way, Eden had already helped Mary considerably. When she arrived in the city, Yeboa welcomed her into his home almost every day, encouraged her in her applications for jobs, and gave her something to occupy her time in the meantime. Eden's lively music and dramatic healing services provided her with at least 10 hours of edifying entertainment each week.

About a month after her arrival Yeboa stopped joking in Mary's presence. At once terrifying and irresistibly attractive, Yeboa's image began to haunt Mary day and night. In Mary's mind her relationship to Yeboa was at this time sexual, and she felt the part of the rejected lover. He seemed to her at once demon and savior, and in confusion she almost left Eden. She returned because of family pressure, and Yeboa soon consolidated his power over her. Her beliefs—about God, Eden, and healing—changed first. Her health and life changed more gradually, but whenever she sinned the Spirit beat her, and when she was sick Yeboa's prayers brought relief.

My relationship to Eden Revival Church was in many ways similar to Mary's, despite my cultural distance from Ghanaian religion. Professors at the University of Ghana brought me into contact with Eden. In March 1969 I had written to Christian Baeta, author of *Prophetism in Ghana:*

> I'm looking forward to an in-depth study of one congregation, with less intensive observations of sister congregations and other churches. Although I want to leave most of my time open to learn and write, I would like to teach one or two hours a day. This would allow me to make a direct contribution, and it might make me more welcome in the congregation. I'll simply offer my services, and perhaps someone in the congregation would allow me to stay as a guest in his home in return.

My letter was shown to Yeboa, he wrote a letter of invitation, and we tentatively agreed that I would study Eden Church and teach part time in Eden Secondary School.

On my third day in Ghana I attended an Eden service. My first dealings were with J. R. Anquandah. A few days later Yeboa, Anquandah, and I agreed on the number of hours I would be teaching—more than I had planned but less than they wanted. I was delighted when Yeboa decided to keep me in his own home, and I moved there a week after my arrival. That Sunday I was introduced in the church service.

For a little over two weeks I stayed virtually all the time in Yeboa's house. My sole occupations were listening to him, talking with the many people who would wait for him there, and studying Twi. I was restless, a bit lonely, but mostly satiated to the point of nausea with religion. During my 50-day trip to Ghana through Asia and east Africa, I had seen so many gods placated in such rapid succession that I had myself lost the ability to pray.

I adopted Yeboa's vegetarian diet, and since fasting seemed so important to him, I decided to try a four-day fast myself. I suffered slight spells of dizziness but was hyperactive intellectually. My dreams became startlingly vivid and revealing. In one dream Yeboa himself appeared as a reassuring figure, while in another he stood at one side as my sister called him a charlatan. On the last day of this fast Yeboa surprised me by singling me out for prayer in church. I did, in fact, feel refreshed and healed. Fasting had made me humbler, more content, and the next several weeks were among the happiest in my life.

After that I allowed Yeboa to bless me routinely during the collection each Sunday, but never had occasion to go forward for healing. A week after the end of my fast Yeboa seemed to be trying to frighten me at the Wednesday night service. He would glare at me, suddenly move as if he were coming toward me, then go elsewhere in the congregation to pray for someone; he surprised several people sitting near me by praying over them, and one after another was "caught by the Spirit." That night was the first time I recorded a completely negative reaction in my notes. I was never entranced.

I continued to spend hour after hour listening to Yeboa, sometimes questioning, but never contradicting. I was intent on learning from him, not just about him. I had false hopes he might change his mind on some issues, astrology for example, through our conversations. On the other side, he thought I might be able to convince Lutheran Church officials to give him money, and he conceived of me as his scribe and propagandist.

I became increasingly eager to turn our lecture sessions into dialogs, and I began to express my opinions more freely, sometimes to Yeboa's annoyance. I found myself becoming bored with long church services, and although I always managed to be present in Eden at least once a week, I no longer attended all of Eden's services. I had been completely cut off from my accustomed social life for four months, and wanted to relax and have fun for a change. I knew mostly Edenians, however, and I was living so close to Yeboa that fear kept many of them, especially women, from associating freely with me.

About two months after my arrival Yeboa began to distrust me. He agreed that as a researcher I ought to sample all shades of opinion about Eden, so I began talking with people who had once been part of Eden but later quit. I was careful to let him know whom I was visiting. At that time I was trying to reconstruct Eden's history, including the circumstances surrounding the court case which resulted in Yeboa's brief imprisonment. Although he did not object, he was not very helpful to me in finding the court records. When I went to Nsawam courthouse one day without telling him in advance, he suspected I might be trying to malign him.

Two and a half months after my arrival I began asking about the finances of the church. I finally asked why no public account is made for Eden's funds, and Yeboa became angry. He accused me of being biased, immature, indiscreet, and of spending too much time with his enemies. He briefly showed me a financial account he gives to the government each year, but saw no reason why he should be accountable to anyone for the gifts people give him.

In the next few days both Anquandah and J. K. Koram talked with me for several hours, and Yeboa and I were partially reconciled. Research continued, but from then on Yeboa and

I talked less frequently and I felt restrained in my investigations. I began to seek American friendship for the first time since leaving the United States. I was less interested in Eden but wanted to fulfill my agreement to teach one term before I left. I fasted for a week shortly before leaving, but this time the resultant energy was channeled into writing more than prayer. I asked Yeboa's special blessing again when I left his house four months after I arrived, and we were at that time at least convinced of each other's good intentions.

I understood him to have agreed to allow me to administer a questionnaire at a Sunday morning service to obtain more accurate information about the general characteristics of the people who come to Eden. I arranged with Yeboa and the choirmaster to administer it to the choir one Saturday night so they could help me give it to the entire congregation the next day. Either Yeboa had not understood what I intended to do or he changed his mind at the last minute, but he decided against allowing the questionnaire after I had already passed copies and pencils to everyone in the choir. He said it would take too much time and violate proper church decorum.

During the next two and a half months I spent about half my time at the library of the University of Ghana, half traveling in Ghana. I visited other spiritual churches, several village festivals, the most important pagan shrine in south Ghana, and more remote areas in north Ghana. By this time my Twi was good enough to enable me to make friends with rural people without an interpreter. I attended a few Eden services, visited the school occasionally, and talked with Yeboa several times. Just before leaving Ghana I visited the Edenians I knew best once more, thanked the whole church, was commended by Koram in an exceptionally free and happy Sunday service, and departed with an exchange of gifts.

Like Mary I had come to Eden upon my arrival in Accra, and most of the people who became my friends were church members. In a little speech to the church when I first arrived I said how much I appreciated the love Edenians seemed to feel for each other and their obvious joy as they sang and danced.

Mary, too, was first attracted by the fellowship and fun. I soon experienced healing in Eden and learned how the Gospel of Christ's power could be a liberating force, especially in Africa. Mary was ill, so for her this discovery was physically compelling.

My conversion was incomplete; I never submitted to Yeboa's personal power. Partly it was because I am a man; while Mary's sexual longings could be transferred to Yeboa, mine sometimes made his house seem almost a prison. My cultural background made me skeptical of religious beliefs Mary took for granted, my role as a researcher kept me analyzing and probing, and my Christian faith kept me from fearing whatever spiritual powers Yeboa might have.

Eden left its impression on me nevertheless. I came to appreciate physical involvement in worship: dancing, ecstatic experience, unabashed bodily contact. Fasting, dreams, and visions opened vistas of a far richer piety than I had known. I am much more impressed with the healing power of prayer, or for that matter, of other intense personal relationships.

Most important, Yeboa taught me to talk about spirits. Like many Americans I am used to looking for patterns in every mystery so as to render it understandable and controllable. I assume that whatever I do not understand could probably be explained by some scientific specialist. If Yeboa had told a mountain to move and it suddenly slid into the sea, I suspect I would have asked him to do it again to decrease the likelihood of coincidental success. In other words, I would not be absolutely convinced of a spiritual power unless it behaved in a regular way so it could be dealt with, not by praying but by manipulation—in which case, although unseen, it would no longer, of course, be a spirit.

These scientific attitudes are fearfully estranged from our raw experience, particularly if we peer out of our urban world of markets and bus schedules. Even such familiar phenomena as wind and rain, tides and earthquakes are not understood or controlled, and what we really feel is much better expressed in literature than science texts. Western man suffers from divided consciousness, and it is only in a novel or perhaps in church that men of a scientific bent dare speak of the totality of existence as we experience it — still something mysterious, out of our control, more like a person than a thing. I still refuse to be restrained by dark spirits and always try to move from mystery to knowledge, but Eden taught me to appreciate the miracles that can always be seen along the way.

On the other hand, my passive presence in Eden Revival Church was not without effect. Contact between Yeboa and Lutheran missionary friends of mine facilitated Eden Revival Church's inclusion in the Ghana Christian Council. J. R. Anquandah's *Eden Revival Church of Ghana Handbook* reflects and responds to some of the thoughts and organization of an early draft of this book. The reorganization of Eden in 1970 probably would have occurred had I never visited Ghana, but the reforms may have been, in part, in reaction to the difficulty I had working under Yeboa's almost absolute authority.

PART III

Summation and Commentary

CHAPTER EIGHT

Dynamics of the Spiritual Church Movement

In the preface five crucial questions were posed. Are these new churches in Ghana similar to Afro-Christian churches elsewhere? Are they rightfully considered part of the Pentecostal movement? What contributions might they make to world Christianity? Is their religious independence connected with political nationalism? How are they related to Ghana's religious heritage? In this final chapter we return to those original questions.

Spiritual Churches and Afro-Christianity

The spiritual churches that have grown up suddenly in Ghana in the last decade are part of a much larger religious tradition, indigenous Afro-Christianity. Few of the leaders of Ghana's new churches realize they have counterparts in all corners of Africa, let alone in the West Indies or the United States, but Afro-Christian churches everywhere are, in fact, remarkably similar.

There were two early attempts to introduce Christianity to Africa. In the first centuries of the Christian era a large number of Africans were converted. Even then some Africans achieved ecclesiastical independence, in the northeast through the Coptic secession and in the northwest through the Donatist "heresy." [1] Missionaries accompanied Portuguese explorers along the coasts of sub-Saharan Africa in the 15th through 17th centuries. They found chiefs who had been baptized still frustratingly independent, intent on maintaining old customs, and willing to abandon the new faith when it no longer brought political advantage.[2] In ancient north Africa and again later along the coasts of sub-Saharan Africa, Christianity virtually disappeared with the political power which had supported it.

The missionization of Africa began again in the 19th century, becoming successful for the first time toward the end of the century with the imposition of European political power. At that juncture a few bold Africans began to withdraw from Christian missions to form the first independent African churches. The leaders who succeeded them in the following decades tended to be less acculturated to colonialism and incorporated more traditional African culture into their churches. Independent African churches have been most prominent in South Africa, Malawi, Kenya, Zaire, and Nigeria. The movement has been suppressed in Portuguese and former French Africa, and it is not strong in predominantly Moslem areas. The general popularity of the movement has continued to accelerate, until now indigenous churches *may* be growing faster than the established churches in most of the countries of sub-Saharan Africa.[3]

Christian missionaries were more quickly welcomed by Afro-Americans in the West Indies. Slaveholders began allowing mission work among slaves in the first half of the 19th century. The great majority of them became at least nominally Christian, and the membership of nearly all denominations in the West Indies is mostly black. The churches which began as missions are, however, generally less important to black people than the myriad Afro-Catholic shrines and indigenous Pentecostal churches. In parts of the West Indies influenced by Roman Catholicism the worship of African deities was often syncretized with the adoration of saints.[4] The same basic pattern is subject to many variations and is called by different names in different locales; the most famous of the Afro-Catholic religions is Haitian *vodun*.

112

Protestant-influenced indigenous churches in the West Indies are even more similar to African indigenous churches. A year after my fieldwork in Ghana I visited several indigenous churches in Guyana, northeast South America. In Guyana, too, I found Christian charismatics and similar types of church organization. I found a theology of law and power — including exorcism and healing, Spirit possession, and an even greater hunger for supernatural knowledge. I found the same extended, exuberant worship, the same colorful uniforms, a related hymnody, and similarly dramatic services and novel sacraments.

In the United States free Negroes founded independent churches in the urban northeast in the late 18th century. These black churches, like the independent churches started by educated Africans a century later, were similar to white churches in form and doctrine. Their founders were simply fed up with being segregated and shoved into the galleries of white churches.

Meanwhile, the slaves in the southeast United States were developing churches like the "Zionist" churches of South Africa or the early prayer churches of west Africa. Much of their African religious heritage, however, was suppressed. After the War Between the States the former slave churches were organized on a large scale, often by northern Negroes. The combination of African-style Christianity with extensive organization was not altogether different from that emerging now in Ghana under the leadership of Eden Revival Church.[5] Even now, although black people in the United States are rapidly becoming urban and secular, descriptions of spiritual churches in Ghana remind many American blacks of their own churches or at least the churches they attended in their childhood in the rural South.

Although the indigenous churches of Africa, the West Indies, and the United States developed independently, many of them share the same characteristics. Long, joyful services, like the all-day festivals of Africa, are a hallmark of black worship. In black churches everybody tends to be involved. Black churches are typically either small or organized into societies, and generally have many minor ecclesiastical offices. The whole congregation often takes time to listen to personal testimonies or to pray for individuals in trouble. Black church leaders are often adept at using elaborate gestures, fixtures, and vestments to create an atmosphere of awe, and black women hurrying to church in white uniforms can be seen in Africa, the West Indies, or the United States on any Sunday morning. Baptism is prominent in many black churches, due partly to white Baptist influence but perhaps also to the importance of water symbolism in African religion. Sacramentals like anointing or sacred objects to be touched are often more commonly used than Holy Communion in black churches.

Music, vocal and instrumental, is the staple of black worship. The songs are short, quickly mastered, and lustily sung. They are almost invariably accompanied by happy hand-clapping and foot-tapping, and often there is also dancing. The spirituals of the United States are famous for their eloquence in expressing the indomitable hope of suffering black people. In Africa little-known composers are writing thousands of spirituals in the same victorious mood. In the West Indies fewer original songs are being written. Instead it is customary in black Pentecostal churches to sing an Anglican hymn or one of the revival songs of Ira D. Sankey, but by the last verse to have rocked the rhythm and jazzed the tune so as to have almost lost the lyrics in a celebration of noisy feet and hands, jamming instruments and voices.

The black charismatic — preacher, healer, diviner — is the organizing principle of Afro-Christianity. A typical black church leader will borrow religious ideas with alacrity, syncretize, invent, and lead his people in surprising directions. If he is as strong as Yeboa-Korie he can dominate his church, or like Isaiah Shembe in South Africa or Father Divine in the United States even become a messiah for his followers. The powerful preacher is a black culture hero. He is at once saint and con-man, and, like Brer Rabbit, he achieves fantastic success with no apparent effort. Kwame Nkrumah and Martin Luther King were only two of the preachers turned politicians who became heroes in the generally antiheroic, plodding course of public affairs.

The theology of Afro-Christianity can be summed up in a

word: power. The Black Power theology of James Cone draws heavily from white sources, but it is true to the spirit of black religion.[6] Traditional African religion's concern for health and success has been carried over into indigenous Afro-Christianity. People come to indigenous churches to be healed, to become fertile, to get a better job or better grades, to have spirit protection from evil around them, to learn the secrets of heaven or the future. They are more likely to dance in celebration than to kneel in contrition, and their hymns, seldom introspective or moralistic, lustily praise God for His victorious might. An African mother seeking help for her sickly baby at Eden Revival Church, a Haitian man at a shrine to get a charm that will enamor his girl friend, a prisoner in the United States seeking racial pride and rehabilitation through the Nation of Islam—these are all images of the quest for life and power that is at the core of Afro-Christianity.

The ethics of Afro-Christianity flow from the experience of God as power, and so the tendency in indigenous black churches throughout the world, as in Eden Revival, is to view morality in terms of obedience. This law-power theology shapes Afro-Christianity's social proclamation. Obedience is sometimes seen as the solution to social problems; the "law and order" approach of Yeboa-Korie is shared by many churchgoing black people in the United States. On the other hand, religious striving for power has sociopolitical results. In Africa indigenous churches have started their own schools, agricultural stations, businesses, even new towns. In the West Indies the economic and political power of indigenous churches has been limited by their bad reputation and occasional illegality.

In the United States the three slave revolts about which we have the most information were all partly inspired by religious leaders.[7] After the War Between the States black churches became their communities' central organizations, with black pastors acting as liaisons to the white power structure. The 20th century brought big urban churches with extensive social welfare organizations, and the emergence of preacher politicians like Adam Clayton Powell, Martin Luther King, and Jesse Jackson. The urban storefront churches may seem otherworldly, but many of them own business enterprises. The two most famous leaders of such churches, Daddy Grace and Father Divine, both established sizable capitalist empires. Contemporary black radicals may be secular in outlook, but their primary constituency is the same class of blacks who might find storefronts attractive. The strut of a man like Huey Newton is directly descended from the black preacher's charismatic demeanor.

Spiritual Churches and Pentecostalism

Afro-Christianity and Pentecostalism are overlapping traditions. Pentecostalism is noted for a number of characteristics: faith healing, spirited music, certain theologies, a typical piety. Its most distinctive trait, however, is speaking in tongues, a stylized form of trance. Other features, its music and faith healing as examples, may also have roots in Africa, but the line of influence can be most easily traced in the case of trance.[8] "Trance" is a technical term meaning simply an altered state of consciousness accompanied by agitation or activity. Some Pentecostals take offense at the use of the word "trance" to describe the "tongues" experience, but no negative connotations are intended; it is necessary to use this neutral word to describe an experience Pentecostals share with people in entirely different religious contexts.

Erika Bourguignon analyzed anthropological data for trance experience and possession belief from societies all over the world and found that, outside the Christian tradition, trance is most frequently interpreted as spirit possession in Africa and areas influenced by Africa. Cults in which trance are sought as evidence of divine presence are prevalent primarily in Africa.[9] The same types of glossolalia found in Pentecostalism are also widespread in Africa.[10]

In contrast, within the Christian tradition there were only a few minor instances of trance attributed to the Holy Spirit before the Second Great Awakening. Trance was cultivated during the Hellenistic period by Christians and others, but during the Middle Ages trance was characteristically interpreted as demon possession. The tradition of Christian mysticism flowered, but mysticism, unlike trance, climaxes in stillness and solitude. Trance interpreted as a sign from the Holy Spirit reappeared centuries later among several marginal groups – the earliest Quakers, the Jansenists and Camisards of 18th-century France, in the early ministry of John Wesley and a few of his co-workers, and among the followers of Ann Lee.[11]

The widespread occurrence of trance during the Second Great Awakening was unprecedented, and it was directly related to the first major successes in evangelism among Afro-American slaves. Large numbers of slaves were being converted for the first time around 1800 in the border states, the area most influenced by the Awakening. A fourth of the memberships of the Baptist and Methodist churches were then black, and those are precisely the churches in which trance became suddenly, shockingly prominent.[12]

Within 30 years genuinely frenzied camp meetings were for the most part a thing of the past, but trance continued among black and some white rural Southerners. The earliest reliable documents of black religion available report the continued practice of trance in black Christian worship after the War Between the States. For example, Miss Elizabeth Kilham, a white schoolteacher, described her visit to "Old Billy's church" for *Putnam's Monthly* in 1870:

> Men stamped, groaned, shouted, clapped their hands; women shrieked and sobbed, two or three tore off their bonnets and threw them across the church, trampled their shawls under foot, and sprang into the air, it seemed almost to their own height, again and again, until they fell exhausted, and were carried to one side, where they lay stiff and rigid like the dead. No one paid them any farther attention, but wilder grew the excitement, louder the shrieks, more violent the stamping, while through and above it all, – over and over again, – each time faster and louder, – rose the refrain, "Jesus said He wouldn't die no more!" [13]

Pentecostalism itself began in 1906 at the Azuza Street Mission, a predominately black congregation in Los Angeles.

The Mission was led by a black preacher, W. J. Seymour, who in turn was a student of C. F. Parham. Parham, a white minister, headed a racially integrated Bible school in Topeka, Kansas. His 40 students were searching for sure evidence of the "baptism of the Holy Ghost." From their study of Acts they concluded that speaking in tongues was the evidence they sought. They prayed for this gift together. The first to receive it was a black girl named Agnes Ozman. Parham and his students preached their discovery in Kansas and then Texas. Seymour went to Los Angeles, where he founded the Azuza Street Mission.

The Azuza revival, graced with glossolalia and other marvelous "signs," continued with vigor for three years. Numerous Baptist and Holiness leaders went to Azuza and returned to their own churches as Pentecostal missionaries. This was true of the Church of God in Christ, a black Wesleyan body which is now the largest Pentecostal church in the world. Scores of zealous evangelists, many of them black, traveled from Azuza to introduce the experience into established congregations or start new congregations. Even today there are hundreds of independent Pentecostal congregations. The Assemblies of God, the largest white Pentecostal church, organized a large part of this disparate movement.[14]

Pentecostalism was most popular among blacks and those whites most likely to have been influenced by blacks. The 1936 census showed that Pentecostals were to be found predominantly among blacks and low-income rural white Southerners.[15] Already in 1908, however, the whites who had been part of the Azuza Street Mission had withdrawn, and in the years that followed white and black Pentecostals throughout the United States separated themselves. Black Pentecostals in the United States often still allow for jumping and dancing in the Spirit, while white Pentecostals have generally become more subdued, limiting themselves to glossolalia.

From the United States, Pentecostalism spread to other parts of the world. T. B. Barratt carried the Pentecostal message from Los Angeles to Norway, and from there it spread through northern Europe. American and European missionaries initiated the movement in South America, Africa, and parts of Asia. Pentecostals have met with amazing success among a wide variety of peoples, but most especially among Africans and Afro-Americans. Not including indigenous African and Afro-American churches, there are 19 countries with more than one percent of their population Pentecostal. All except Chile, El Salvador, and Sweden are in Africa or include large numbers of Afro-Americans.[16]

In addition, Pentecostal missionaries have catalyzed indigenous Afro-Christianity. Trance was native to Africa, but the Biblical argument which allowed for it in a Christian context was C. F. Parham's invention. The indigenous Pentecostal ("Zionist") movement of southern Africa was sparked by missionaries associated with the Apostolic Faith Mission who arrived in 1908. Trance as evidence of the Holy Spirit was introduced to west Africa by the Apostolic Church, a Welsh Pentecostal group, which supervised indigenous churches in Nigeria and Ghana in the 1930's; they had practiced faith healing and revelatory visions, but speaking in tongues and other trance experience became part of their piety during their association with the Apostolic Church. This study has also demonstrated a continuing, intermittent but influential, contact between Pentecostal churches, including the African Israel Church Nineveh, Canadian Pentecostal Mission introduced Christian trance to east Africa in 1919; several of the original indigenous Pentecostal churches, including the African Israel Church Ninevah, began as secessions from that mission. More recently organized indigenous churches which practice trance may have imitated these predecessors. The practice of "shaking" in the Republic of Congo and Zaire was derived from traditional religion, but Pentecostal missions, also popular, may have had some influence on the way trance is understood and practiced in these indigenous churches.[17]

In the Caribbean region trance was practiced among nominal Christians at Afro-Catholic shrines long before the introduction of Pentecostalism. The origins of most indigenous Pentecostal groups — called "Shakers," "spiritual Baptists," "Jordanites," and yet other names in other places—are obscure, but many claim to have originated in Pentecostal missions. The Caribbean region has been influenced by Pentecostal missionaries, literature, and radio broadcasts since the beginning of the movement in the United States. Indigenous leaders, even if repudiated by most local Pentecostal missionaries, turn to other missionaries, Pentecostal magazines and tracts from the United States, or mission radio broadcasts for inspiration.

Is Eden Revival an indigenous Afro-Christian church or is it part of the Pentecostal movement? It is both, because Pentecostalism is, in large part, an Afro-Christian phenomenon! Its origins are, in large part, among Afro-Americans, and it has grown, in large part, in those areas of the world influenced by Africa. The lines between Pentecostal missions and indigenous churches are seldom clearly drawn, because Pentecostal missionaries usually push toward early self-government on the part of their churches and churches which are apparently indigenous have often successfully applied for aid from missionaries.

Including indigenous African Pentecostal churches there are probably 25 countries with over one percent of their citizens Pentecostal, 22 of which are in Africa or include large numbers of Afro-Americans in their populations.[18] Statistical information about indigenous Pentecostals in the Caribbean region is virtually nonexistent, but if their numbers were known, perhaps other Caribbean countries would have to be numbered with the 25. Pentecostalism in Africa and among Afro-Americans has grown as verdantly as a hothouse plant returned to its natural environment.

Spiritual Churches and Future Christianity

It might be said that the apostle Paul was the first indigenous church leader. Christianity began as a movement among Jews, nearly confined to Jerusalem. Paul dared preach Christ Jesus to Gentile peoples, adapting the Christian message to new cultures, even abandoning clear legal injunctions in the Scriptures for the sake of his Gospel, and leaving infant congregations on their own after only brief missionary visits.

In the next several centuries, particularly after it was officially wedded to the Roman Empire, Christianity was shaped by Hellenistic culture. During a second great missionary movement, heavily influenced by medieval power politics, northern Europe was converted to Christianity. The outcropping of sects in Asia, Africa, and the Americas now that the modern colonial era is coming to an end, is reminiscent of the Protestant Reformation of the 16th century. The final dissolution of the Holy Roman Empire and the rise of nation states in Europe at that time was also accompanied by ecclesiastical rebellions against imperial control and the translation of religion into local languages and cultural forms. The first Protestant movements have in turn given rise to hundreds of independent churches for various classes, ethnic groups, and localities in Europe and the United States.

Still, since the Moslem conquests of the seventh and eighth centuries, Christianity has been almost exclusively a European religion. Most of its variations remain within the spectrum of European culture. In the 19th century, as Europe came to dominate the world, Christian missionaries were sent out with entrepreneurs, colonists, armies, and administrators. Christianity's third great missionary impulse took advantage of Europe's economic, political, and cultural expansiveness.

That wave seems to have subsided. Two world wars convinced former colonial peoples that their masters were not destined to rule, and tempered the cultural arrogance of white people. The last 20 years have been characterized by the reclamation of political self-determination by many former colonies and by efforts toward economic liberation. Simultaneously, many Europeans and Americans have become markedly pessimistic about their own culture, and what was formerly considered "primitive" in art and religion has suddenly become popular.

Formerly missionized peoples all over the world have reacted to oppression by forming indigenous churches, especially now that the political domination of the United States and Europe is beginning to be relaxed. The Taiping Rebellion and other semi-Christian groups in China, the Cargo Cults in Melanesia, and the American Native Church (commonly called the peyote cult) among American Indians are widely known examples of reaction to oppression in the form of a radically indigenous Christianity. The largest Protestant church in the Philippines today is the *Iglesia ni Cristo,* an independent Filipino sect which has grown wildly since Philippine independence. In some respects it is like African independent churches: services in the native language (Tagalog), heightened emotion, charismatic and authoritarian leadership, strict discipline, and intense fellowship. In Japan, too, the fastest growing religions are those which were recently invented. These new religions, notably *Soka Gakkai* and *Rissho Kosei Kai,* are in part a reaction to Japan's defeat in World War II. They combine elements of Buddhism and Shintoism with parts of Christianity and secular humanism. They, too, tend to be intense and disciplined groups, usually with a charismatic founder still in charge.

Afro-Christian indigenous churches, including those in Ghana, are part of this transformation. Africans and Europeans alike are more respectful of African culture now than they were 20 years ago. Many missionaries have been recalled, and those who remain are almost all keenly aware that African churches should be self-supporting and self-directed. A number of the new missionaries from the United States are working primarily with indigenous churches, rather than trying to organize groups of their own. When foreign religious leaders or missionaries visit Brother Yeboa, they nearly always come to listen rather than lecture. The Roman Catholic Church in Ghana has attempted to be as African in leadership and style as possible, and the large Protestant churches, the Presbyterians and Methodists, are intent on full ecclesiastical independence. Eden Revival Church has been admitted to the Christian Council of Ghana, and other indigenous churches will soon follow.

African Christianity, especially in its indigenous forms, has much to recommend it to people outside Africa too. Bible passages which are exegetical problems for many Europeans and Americans are perfectly understandable to Africans. The rationalistic theology and bureaucratic organization of Western

Christendom cannot rival these churches in fervor, openness to the supernatural, or richness of piety. Their emphasis is on experience — community, morality, healing, visions, singing, and dancing — rather than abstract ideas. As Christians live out their faith in "the one holy catholic and apostolic Church," those in Europe and the United States may find themselves still contributing money and technical expertise, but now also receiving religious advice. Missionaries from Africa working in European and North American churches are at least as appropriate as missionaries to Africa.

Indigenous African churches will probably have their greatest effect through their influence on other churches in Africa, but indigenous churches have already had considerable direct influence outside Africa too. One avenue of influence is their relationship to American and European Pentecostal groups and the visits of African indigenous churchmen to the United States and Europe. Another is their acceptance by international ecumenical associations, like the World Council of Churches. Most significant, they have inspired a burgeoning literature, over 2,200 books and articles. About 100 additional items are being published each year, an indication of the worldwide interest Africa's indigenous churches have generated.[19]

Spiritual Churches and Political Nationalism

The posture of African independent churches has often been nationalistic. For example, a publication of Eden Revival Church boasted:

> There is nothing exotic about Eden. All is Ghanaian and African — the Leadership, the Membership, the Music, the Service. It is a spontaneous and indigenous development, the direct work of the Holy Spirit alone, deriving its sources from the heart and mind of one man, Brother Yeboa-Korie.[20]

The independent churches draw sustenance from widespread impatience with white paternalism and a renewed confidence in African culture. The independent churches, in Ghana as elsewhere, are the religious counterpart of political nationalism.

Political independence has facilitated religious independence, and the two movements have prospered together. Political independence in former French colonies has finally allowed indigenous Christian prophets there to begin public work. Zaire nationalism brought various cults together into the *Église de Jésus-Christ sur la terre par le prophète Simon Kimbangu,* now a member organization of the World Council of Churches.[21] In Kenya scores of new groups, including several with memberships of over 50,000 have appeared since national independence.[22] The churches of west Africa have also grown tremendously. Mitchell reports a threefold growth in the number of prayer churches in Ibadan, Nigeria, in the 1950's.[23] There were only a handful of spiritual churches in Ghana before political independence in 1957; now drumming and spiritual songs can be heard in most parts of Accra any Wednesday or Friday night.

Nevertheless, the relationship between independent churches and nationalism has been ambiguous. Surprisingly, the African churches have seldom lent their strength to the struggle for political independence. The independent churches of the 19th and early 20th centuries were in tune with the progressive African opinion of their day, but they certainly did not advocate political independence. Although articulate Africans objected to colonial abuses, even the radicals of that time welcomed the colonial system itself. Welbourne has shown that Mugema's Society of the One Almighty God, which drew over a tenth of the Baganda into its membership in 1914–21, was an ecclesiastical rebellion against the same oligarchy that had usurped political power, but even in that case, the conscious motives of the schism leaders were purely theological.[24]

African prophets have shared visions of heaven or a millennium where oppression of Africans would end, but such messages are cathartic, not revolutionary. Independent religious movements led to anti-European violence in a few instances, most of them in central Africa, but even in these cases the violence was romantic, unorganized, and ineffective. The famous Nyasaland Uprising in 1915, for example, accomplished little beyond the murder of a particularly odious plantation owner, but resulted

124

in the slaughter of over 50 Africans.[25] With a few exceptions,[26] African independent churches throughout their history have fed on resentment against the white man's domination in Africa, have liberated themselves ecclesiastically from white rule, but have not been instrumental in achieving political and economic independence.

Ironically, a number of the "independent churches" of Ghana might almost be called "neocolonial churches." The colonial period ended, for the most part, in one short decade because the European political, economic, and ecclesiastical empires had overreached themselves. The political independence of the colonies was granted quickly, especially by England, because it relieved the European powers of the responsibilities of government. European monopolies, already firmly entrenched, have not lost their grip on Africa, however. They often have more assets than the new nations they exploit. While the nations of Africa which allow the big companies complete freedom or even special privileges prosper, at the same time they forfeit genuine independence. The term "neocolonialism" refers to this more subtle but usually quite effective type of foreign domination. Nationalistic African governments have achieved a great deal of independence, of course, but their maneuvering space is limited by foreign economic pressures.

For the United States the political independence of the underdeveloped nations has meant easier access to their markets. The most advanced technology is now centered in the United States, so Americans have been able to encroach on formerly European territory. In Africa the American presence is still comparatively small and often disguised behind French and British companies, but politically independent Africa has turned noticeably toward the new center of power in this neocolonial era.

Ghana shifted toward the United States in its policies after the coup that overthrew Nkrumah early in 1966. Throughout the late colonial period Ghana was exporting more than it was importing from the United States. Exports to the United States in 1949 – 56 averaged 22% of total exports, while imports averaged 5% of total imports.[27] The surplus dollars were exported to Britain to help that nation's balance of payments problem.[28] Under Nkrumah the Ghanaian economy was oriented toward the USSR and eastern Europe instead of Britain. The imbalance with regard to the United States was only slightly changed, imports growing to around 8% a year just before the coup.[29] But in the year of the coup imports from the United States jumped from 9% to 17%. The new economic situation was accompanied by a corresponding reorientation toward the United States politically.

Something of the same sort of mechanism is at work in the churches. Missionaries have been among the least grasping and most accessible white men in Africa. In general, Africans understandably tried to get as much material help and knowledge about Europe as possible from the missionaries. Now most support from Europe has been withdrawn, but the United States is currently spending about $320 million annually for missionary work.[30] Compared to American business American missions are a paltry operation, but compared to Ghanaian churches their financial resources are great. They also offer effective personnel and ideas about theology, music, and organization that some Ghanaians find attractive.

Several of the most successful Ghanaian spiritual churches have received substantial aid from the United States. Even some tiny churches that have almost no chance of attracting American mission help seem to be straining in that direction. The newly founded Ghanaian churches are indigenous in leadership, worship, and doctrine. They are much less subject to foreign influence than the Ghanaian churches of twenty years ago. Their independence is real and should not be underemphasized. Eden Revival Church has probably been influenced by Americans as much as any of them, and Yeboa is certainly subject to no one. He has, however, been gradually affected by his contacts with Americans, and Eden definitely shows the marks of foreign influence.

Neocolonialism substitutes influence and voluntary dependence for direct control and servitude, not only in politics and economics but also in religion. Particularly since the coup in 1966 Ghana's government has tried to attract foreign capitalists, particularly Americans. Similarly, Ghana's spiritual churches now seek out foreign missionaries, particularly Americans. In seeking aid from Americans, spiritual churches have not lost their self-confidence or their self-determination, but American missions have in the process perceptibly modified the course of the spiritual church movement.

Spiritual Churches
and Ghana's Religious Heritage

The contemporary spiritual church movement is an organic extension of Ghana's religious history. It has grown naturally out of precolonial religion, earlier forms of Christianity, and the medicine shrines.

From precolonial religion the spiritual churches have inherited the quest of African religion for power. Dancing, healing, supernatural knowledge, the luster of personality traits associated with the prophet—all these things are part of the traditional African religious concern for vitality. The spiritual churches do not worship small gods or ancestors, but the use of charms or amulets is continued with a different theological explanation in the use of holy water, blessed handkerchiefs, and candles.

Spiritual churches also perpetuate some elements of the fervent Christianity the first missionaries brought to Ghana. Yeboa recalls with approval the forcefulness of the early Basel missionaries. Later missionaries were not as faithful to their predecessors as the Africans who seceded from the missions at the turn of the century. When the later missionaries stalled earlier plans for the independence of the African churches, a few Africans seceded. Those first schisms prepared the way for larger independent churches later.

Christianity grew suddenly in the years 1910–30. Since most of the new converts heard about Christianity from African evangelists, the mission churches must have had an African flavor from the outset. There were not enough missionaries in the country to adequately indoctrinate all those converts until at least 1930. A number of completely African spiritual churches were formed in 1910–30, but during those years even the mission churches must have been led, for the most part, by Africans. Missionaries in Ghana even applauded the work of African prophets, powerful preachers like William Wade Harris, who were entirely independent of mission control.

The growth of the "medicine shrines" after 1930 was in part a reaction to the increasingly disciplined European orthodoxy of the missions. The medicine shrines borrowed a few ideas from the churches, but their growth reflected disillusionment with European government and religion. The spiritual churches also respond to the widespread desire for African-led religion, healing, divining, and an African mode of worship. The organization of a modern spiritual church—an inner "family," a larger core of regular members, and thousands of occasional supplicants—is borrowed directly from the medicine shrines. Finally, the cosmopolitan pragmatism of African religion, represented by the wholesale importation of new "medicines" in the 1930's and 1940's, also remains part of the spiritual church heritage.

Political nationalism brought an end to ecclesiastical domination, and the modern African churches that emerged in the 1950's were to some extent molded by Nkrumah's religious politics. They were also influenced by Nigerian prayer churches and comparatively wealthy American revivalistic missions.

During the 1960's, particularly the last half of the decade, the spiritual church movement suddenly grew more quickly, becoming the most dynamic element in Ghanaian religion. Countless influences converge on any social evolution of this scale, but in view of the parallels between religious and economic shifts in Ghana's past, it is reasonable to suspect that the economic woes of the 1960's were one factor in this accelerated growth.

Optimism was high in the 1950's. Cocoa, the mainstay of Ghana's economy, was being sold at higher and higher prices each year. The colony moved rapidly toward independence; the new government then revolutionized the educational system, made modern medical care much more available, and initiated impressive development projects, notably the magnificent Volta Dam and Tema Harbor.

In the early 1960's the cocoa price started falling, some of Nkrumah's massive debt began to come due, Ghana suffered trade deficits, imports were severely restricted, and prices inflated (the Accra price index rose nearly five percent per annum 1960—63), further shrinking the average Ghanaian's buying power. The economic situation progressively worsened, until by 1966 the real income of an Accra worker was lower than it had been at any time since 1938.[31]

The National Liberation Council's coup in 1966 finally obliterated the high hopes Nkrumah had inspired. They virtually declared national bankruptcy, and Western powers celebrated Nkrumah's downfall by granting extensions on their loans. The price of cocoa jumped suddenly, and some infant government-owned industries were sold to European and American capitalists. These emergency measures rescued Ghana—at least in the short run—from economic disaster, but deflationary policies threw thousands of formerly employed men out of work, and the national debt continued to rise. The devastating drop in the standard of living and expectations in the mid-1960's may well have inspired another religious search.

Already in 1960 6.5% of the male labor force, 12.1% of the male labor force aged 15—29, was unemployed.[32] The frequent complaint Field reported from men at an Ashanti shrine, "I am not prospering,"[33] was even then well justified. And since the mid-1960's job opportunities have become much worse. Government policies aimed at stopping inflation have greatly increased unemployment. One connection between this recession and the spiritual churches is certain: Many ambitious young men have entered the spiritual church business in desperation, multiplying the number of sects and adding their force to the movement.

Financial trauma provided occasion for religious change, but why did spiritual churches expand at the expense of medicine shrines in the 1960's? One likely cause was a rapid increase in the availability of school education. Between 1950 and 1963—64 the number of children in public schools at the primary and secondary levels increased almost sixfold. Nkrumah made primary education free and compulsory 1961 – 62, and in one year alone the number of students in schools approximately doubled! [34] Because education has always been so closely associated with the missions in Ghana, educated people tend to be ashamed to be seen at medicine shrines. Because the Bible is central to spiritual churches, educated people who would not openly go to a "heathen" shrine do not lose respect if they are noticed at a spiritual church service. They can receive spiritual help from a Christian prophet as well as from a shrine priest, worship in a way that satisfies their deepest needs, but not forfeit the status associated with education and Christianity. [35]

The expansion of enrollment in the early 1960's could only begin to have effect after those students had been in school a few years, so that this may very well be the crucial factor in the move from shrines to spiritual churches in the late 1960's. Significantly, the core groups of many spiritual churches, Eden for example, are young and comparatively well-educated.

The acceleration of the spiritual church movement can be seen as the naturally quickening spread of a good idea. Spiritual churches are growing because they meet many people's needs. They are taking the particular form they have because it best satisfies the religious longings of many modern Ghanaians. The movement has a dynamic of its own, and no leader is powerful enough to control it. Rather the power of individual leaders flows from the movement and is shaped by it. Yeboa, for example, resisted several crucial developments in Eden, but he could not have refused his followers without losing them.

Nearly half of all Ghanaians call themselves Christians. The impact of schools and missions has been too deep in the lives of many families for them to abandon Christianity. Yet many of these people still seek spiritual power – healthy babies, good jobs, protection from all sorts of evil. Many second- and third-generation Christians still like dancing and drumming, the spontaneity and exuberance of African worship. Many still crave the close communal fellowship of village life and religion.

The spiritual churches are undeniably Christian, but they also have power. When someone lunges and rolls in an Eden service, no one can doubt that Yeboa has power; yet he is doing it in the name of Christ. Spiritual church services, like village festivals, are extended celebrations. Their symbolism, in the west African tradition, is syncretistic, and their hymns are indigenous, fresh, and easy to learn. They are either small enough for everybody to know each other, or are divided like Eden into small fellowships. Some of them like Eden are strictly disciplined and can help people, alcoholics for example, who need firmer moral grounding.

The longings of traditional religion, unrest with a foreign Christianity, and the sense of shame many people feel in visiting a medicine shrine are all resolved together in the spiritual churches. It took a few years, the encouragement of missions from Nigeria and abroad, and the leadership of some young Ghanaians; but once the movement was under way, every year more and more people joined it because of its intrinsic worth.

Footnotes

Preface

1. David B. Barrett, *Schism and Renewal in Africa* (London, 1968), pp. 72, 79.

2. David B. Barrett, "A. D. 2000: 350 Million Christians in Africa," *International Review of Missions,* 59 (1970), 39 – 53.

3. David M. Beckmann, "Trance: From Africa to Pentecostalism," *CTM,* XLV, 1 (January 1974), 11 – 26.

4. Ione Acquah, *Accra Survey* (London, 1958), p. 145.

5. Margaret J. Field, *Search for Security* (London, 1960), p. 36.

Chapter One

1. R. Sutherland Rattray, *Religion and Art in Ashanti* (London, 1927); Margaret J. Field, *Religion and Medicine of the Ga People* (London, 1937).

2. Margaret J. Field, *Search for Security* (London, 1960), p. 49.

3. Rattray, p. 138.

4. Walter Birmingham, I. Neustadt, E. N. Omaboe, *A Study of Contemporary Ghana: The Economy of Ghana,* I (London, 1967), 132.

5. Cited by F. L. Bartels, *The Roots of Ghana Methodism* (Cambridge, England, 1965), p. 13.

6. C. P. Groves, *The Planting of Christianity in Africa, 1914 – 54,* IV (London, 1958), 358 – 59.

7. Philip Curtin, *The Image of Africa* (Madison, Wis., 1964), pp. 150 – 70.

8. Max Warren, *Social History and Christian Mission* (London, 1967), pp.45 – 50.

9. Hans Jacob Cnattingius, *Bishops and Societies* (London, 1952), pp. 231 – 32.

10. Christopher Fyfe, *A History of Sierra Leone* (London, 1962), p. 139.

11. K. A. Opoku, "A History of Independent Churches in Ghana, 1862 – 1969" (unpublished paper).

12. Robert R. Clark, "An Appeal to Our Universities on Behalf of the Heathen and Mohammedan World," *The Church Missionary Intelligencer,* VI (London, 1871), 46.

13. E. A. Ayandele, *The Missionary Impact on Modern Nigeria* (London, 1966), pp. 212–29; James Bertin Webster, *The African Church Among the Yoruba 1888–1922* (London, 1964), pp. 7–20; Bengt G. M. Sundkler, *Bantu Prophets in South Africa* (London, 1961), pp. 24–41.

14. Cited by Opoku.

15. M. J. Marshall, *Christianity and Nationalism in Ghana* (unpublished thesis, Institute of African Studies, University of Ghana, 1965), pp. 103–104.

16. Frank E. K. Amoah, *Accra: A Study of the Development of a West African City* (unpublished thesis, Institute of African Studies, University of Ghana, 1964), p. 68.

17. Christian G. Baeta, "Aspects of Religion," in *A Study of Contemporary Ghana: Some Aspects of Social Structure*, ed. Walter Birmingham et al., II (London, 1967), 249.

18. James P. Dretke, *A Study of Moslems in Accra* (unpublished thesis, Institute of African Studies, University of Ghana, 1965).

19. Presbyterian Church of Ghana, *Report for 1968* (Accra, 1968), p. 9; The Methodist Church of Ghana, *Conference Schedules for 1967–68* (unpublished, Office of the Synod Clerk, The Methodist Church of Ghana, Accra, Ghana). A third of Ghana's Methodists are children.

20. Consultation on the Healing Ministry of the Church, "Findings and Questions," *The Ghana Bulletin of Theology*, 3, 2–3 (December 1967), 28.

21. *Statistical Handbook of the Republic of Ghana 1967* (Central Bureau of Statistics, Accra), p. 13.

22. *The Gold Coast Annual: Year Book of the Wesleyan Church on the Gold Coast, West Africa, 1910* (Cape Coast, Ghana, 1912), p. 31; *The Gold Coast Annual 1940* (Cape Coast, 1941), p. 30. Statistics on Catholic growth would fill a serious gap in this discussion of colonialism and Christianity.

23. Sundkler, p. 48; F. B. Welbourne, *East African Christian* (Ibadan, 1965), p. 147; Vittorio Lanternari, trans. Lisa Sergio, *The Religions of the Oppressed* (New York, 1963), p. 29. Cf. esp. Marie-Louise Martin, *Kirche ohne Weisse* (Basel, 1971).

24. W. J. Platt, *An African Prophet* (London, 1934), pp. 42–61; Gordon M. Haliburton, *The Prophet Harris* (New York, 1973), pp. 71–90.

25. Robert T. Parsons, *The Churches and Ghana Society* (Leiden, 1963), p. 6.

26. Christian G. Baeta, *Prophetism in Ghana* (London, 1962), pp. 6–27.

27. Michael Crowder, *West Africa Under Colonial Rule* (London, 1968), pp. 254–70.

28. Kwamina B. Dickson, *A Historical Geography of Ghana* (Cambridge, England, 1964), pp. 176–77.

29. Ibid., p. 177.

30. The Methodist Church—Gold Coast, *Annual Report 1921*, p. 9.

31. Baeta, *Prophetism in Ghana*, pp. 29 – 43.

32. Opoku.

33. Baeta, *Prophetism in Ghana*, pp. 68 – 69.

34. Ione Acquah, *Accra Survey* (London, 1958), p. 143.

35. Field, *Search for Security*, p. 90.

36. Jack Goody, "Anomie in Ashante?" *Africa*, XXVII (London, 1957), 359.

37. Goody, p. 361.

38. D. K. Fiawoo, "From Cult to Church: A Study of Some Aspects of Religious Change in Ghana," *Ghana Journal of Sociology*, IV, 2 (October 1968), 80.

39. Barbara Ward E., "Some Observations on Religious Cults in Ashanti," *Africa*, XXVI (London, 1956), 52.

40. *The Gold Coast Annual 1900*, p. 14; *1912*, p. 13; *1921*, p. 26; *1941*, p. 30; *1951*, p. 19; *Minutes of the Gold Coast District Synod and Missionary Meeting 1930*, p. 30; *The Methodist Church of Ghana Annual Report 1961* (unpublished material in the office of the Synod Clerk, The Methodist Church of Ghana, Accra, Ghana).

41. Acquah, p. 146.

42. The Methodist Church of Ghana, *Conference Schedules 1961 – 68;* Presbyterian Church of Ghana, *Reports 1960 – 68.*

43. The Methodist Church of Ghana, *Conference Schedule 1967 – 68;* unpublished material in the Office of the Synod Clerk, Presbyterian Church of Ghana.

44. Baeta, "Aspects of Religion," p. 249.

Chapter Two

1. Ione Acquah, *Accra Survey* (London, 1958), p. 145.

2. Christian G. Baeta, *Prophetism in Ghana* (London, 1962), pp. 76 – 83.

3. Bob Fitch and Mary Oppenheimer, *Ghana: End of an Illusion* (New York and London, 1966), p. 25.

4. George Bennett, "Christianity and African Nationalism," *Mawazo*, I, 3 (June 1968), 65.

5. Ibid., p. 64.

6. Christian G. Baeta, "Aspects of Religion," in *A Study of Contemporary Ghana: Some Aspects of Social Structure*, ed. Walter Birmingham et al., II (London, 1967), 249.

7. James Bertin Webster, *The African Church Among the Yoruba 1888 – 1922* (London, 1964); J. D. Y. Peel, *Aladura: A Religious Movement Among the Yoruba* (London, 1968).

8. *The Gold Coast 1931: Appendices Containing Comparative Returns and General Statistics of the 1931 Census* (Accra, 1932), p. 21; *The Gold Coast:*

Census of Population 1948 Report and Tables (London, 1950), p. 18; B. Gil, A. F. Aryee, and D. K. Ghansah, *1960 Population Census of Ghana: Special Report "E," Tribes in Ghana* (Accra, 1964), p. 4, 45.

9. Acquah, p. 148.

10. Hans W. Debrunner, *A History of Christianity in Ghana* (Accra, 1968).

11. John V. Taylor, "Christianity in Africa," in *Africa: A Handbook to the Continent,* ed. Colin Legum (London, 1961), p. 467.

12. Bengt G. M. Sundkler, *Bantu Prophets in South Africa* (London, 1961).

13. F. B. Welbourne, *East African Christian* (Ibadan, 1965), p. 147.

14. R. L. Wishlade, *Sectarianism in Southern Nyasaland* (London, 1965), pp. 14 – 15.

15. Peel, pp. 105 – 12.

16. Edwin and Irene Weaver, *The Uyo Story* (Elkhart, Ind., 1970).

17. Moses Jehu-Appiah, in a letter to the author dated June 21, 1970.

Chapter Three

1. K. A. Opoku, "The Universal Prayer Group – 'Mpaebo Kuw' (Adoagyiri, Nsawam) – The Call of the Prophet," *Institute of African Studies Research Review,* V, 1 (Michaelmas Term 1968), 101 – 108.

2. Christian G. Baeta, *Prophetism in Ghana* (London, 1962), pp. 29 – 30.

3. James Anquandah, "Brother Yeboa-Korie and the Eden Revival Church," *The Edenian,* I, 1 (January-February 1968), 3.

4. S. R. Ntiforo and P. Rutishauser, "Prayer Groups and Sects" (Accra, 1966), p. 8.

5. Ibid.

6. J. R. Anquandah, "Panorama," *The Torch,* I, 4 (October 1968), 8.

7. Bob Fitch and Mary Oppenheimer, *Ghana: End of an Illusion* (New York and London, 1966), pp. 41, 55.

8. "African Christian Needs New Awakening," *Mirror* (Jan. 23, 1966), p. 4.

9. "Christian Council Speaks," *Mirror* (Feb. 6, 1966), p. 14.

Chapter Four

1. Efraim Andersson, *Churches at the Grass Roots: A Study in Congo-Brazzaville* (New York, 1962), p. 154.

2. Margaret J. Field, *Search for Security* (London, 1960), p. 52.

3. "Exit King '67," *The Edenian,* I, 1 (January-February 1968), 2.

4. J. R. Anquandah, "Editorial," *The Torch,* I, 3 (June 1968), 1.

5. Hans W. Debrunner, *Witchcraft in Ghana* (Accra, 1961), pp. 19 – 60.

6. Charles Yeboa-Korie, "Christian Spiritual Development," *The Torch*, I, 3 (June 1968), 3.

Chapter Five

1. S. R. Ntiforo and P. Rutishauser, "Prayer Groups and Sects" (Accra, 1966), p. 8.
2. H. O. Beeko, choir director of the Eden Revival Church in Accra, selected 81 of Eden's most commonly sung hymns. Analysis of these favorite hymns revealed 47 of the 81 were simple praise songs (9 exclamations of general praise, 15 celebrating God's strength, and 23 praising God's goodness, about half of those speaking of some sort of immediate aid and half of forgiveness and eternal life). Eleven were petitions, most of them asking for God's help in very general terms. Seven described the Christian's utter dependence on God. Only 16 dealt at all with human responsibility. Two exhorted the worshipers to love, two to evangelize, one to work hard, and one to obey parents; the rest speak of faithfulness and obedience in general terms like "following Jesus," "obeying His laws," or "staying by Jesus' side". This is remarkably similar to the content of hymns sung by the Church of the Lord (Aladura), according to H. W. Turner, *African Independent Church: The Life and Faith of the Church of the Lord (Aladura)*, II (London, 1967), 301, 309.

Chapter Seven

1. Fifty-two percent of the Accra population over 15 years old has not been to school according to the *1960 Census Special Report A: Statistics of Large Towns* (Ghana Census, 1960), Part 3.

Chapter Eight

1. John V. Taylor, "Christianity in Africa," in *Africa: A Handbook to the Continent*, ed. Colin Legum (London, 1961), p. 465; F. B. Welbourne, *East African Rebels* (London, 1961), p. 42.

2. Vittorio Lanternari, trans. Lisa Sergio, *The Religions of the Oppressed* (New York, 1963), p. 8.

3. David B. Barrett, *Schism and Renewal in Africa* (London, 1968), p. 66.

4. Melville J. Herskovits, *The New World Negro* (Bloomington, Ind., 1966), pp. 321–53.

5. E. Franklin Frazier, *The Negro Church in America* (New York, 1964), pp. 30–31.

6. James H. Cone, *A Black Theology of Liberation* (Philadelphia and New York, 1970).

7. John H. Bracey Jr., August Meier, and Elliot Rudwick, eds., *American Slavery: The Question of Resistance* (Belmont, Calif., 1971), pp. 21–36, 160–77.

8. David M. Beckmann, "Trance: From Africa to Pentecostalism," *CTM*, XLV, 1 (January 1974), 11–26.

9. Erika Bourguignon, "World Distribution and Patterns of Possession States," in *Trance and Possession States*, ed. Raymond Prince (Montreal, 1968), pp. 3–34.

10. L. Carlyle May, "A Survey of Glossolalia and Related Phenomena in Non-Christian Religions," *American Anthropologist*, XLVIII (1956), 75–93.

11. E. Glenn Hinson, "A Brief History of Glossolalia," in *Glossolalia*, by Frank Stagg, E. Glenn Hinson, and Wayne E. Oates (Nashville and New York, 1967), pp. 45–56; R. A. Knox, *Enthusiasm* (Oxford, 1950), pp. 71–116, 241, 356–73, 520–35; John Wesley, *Journal*, ed. Nehemiah Curnock, II (London, 1938), 180 ff.

12. Beckmann, pp. 17–19.

13. Bruce Jackson, ed., *The Negro and His Folklore in Nineteenth Century Periodicals* (Austin and London, 1967), pp. 127–28.

14. Walter J. Hollenweger, *The Pentecostals* (Minneapolis, 1972), pp. 21–46; James S. Tinney, "Black Origins of the Pentecostal Movement," *Christianity Today*, XVI, 1 (Oct. 8, 1971), 4–6.

15. Hollenweger, *The Pentecostals*, p. 26.

16. *World Christian Handbook* (Nashville and New York, 1967); Walter J. Hollenweger, *Handbuch der Pfingstbewegung* (Geneva, 1966–67).

17. Bengt Sundkler, *Bantu Prophets in South Africa* (London, 1961), pp. 47–50; F. B. Welbourne, *East African Christian* (Ibadan, 1965), p. 147; Efraim Andersson, *Messianic Popular Movements in the Lower Congo* (Uppsala, 1958), pp. 52, 109.

18. Barrett, pp. 78–79.

19. Ibid, p. 39.

20. James Anquandah, "Brother Yeboa-Korie and the Eden Revival Church," *The Edenian*, I, 1 (January-February 1968), 4.

21. Lanternari, pp. 24–31.

22. F. B. Welbourne and B. A. Ogot, *A Place to Feel at Home* (London, 1966), pp. 52–69.

23. Robert Mitchell, "The Aladura in Ibadan" (presented to the Social Science Seminar, University College, Ibadan, March, 1962), p. 8.

24. Welbourne, *East African Rebels*, pp. 3–20.

25. George Shepperson and Thomas Price, *Independent African* (Edinburgh, 1961), pp. 265–320.

26. Welbourne, *East African Rebels*, pp. 3–20, describes several churches in Kenya and Uganda affiliated with Marcus Garvey's Universal Negro Improvement Association. Geoffrey Parrinder, *Religion in an African City* (London, 1953), pp. 126–28, discusses two churches founded for political

reasons in Nigeria in the 1940's. Christian G. Baeta, *Prophetism in Ghana* (London, 1962), mentions that Jehu Appiah, leader of the *Musamo Disco Cristo* Church, was a marginal figure in the Ghanaian independence movement. John V. Taylor and Dorothea Lehmann, *Christians of the Copperbelt* (Liverpool and London, 1961), pp. 155, 166, list several congregational schisms with political motivations. These cases, however, were exceptional.

27. The Office of the Government Statistician, *Digest of Statistics,* V (Gold Coast, 1956), 1–2.

28. Bob Fitch and Mary Oppenheimer, *Ghana: End of an Illusion* (New York and London, 1966), pp. 40–52.

29. Central Bureau of Statistics, *Quarterly Digest of Statistics,* XV (Ghana, 1966), 2; XVIII (Ghana, 1968), 2.

30. J. B. A. Kessler, "Let's Spend Mission Dollars More Wisely," *World Vision,* 13, 5 (May 1969), 4.

31. Walter Birmingham et al., *A Study of Contemporary Ghana: The Economy of Ghana,* I (London, 1967), 26–29.

32. Ibid., I, 149.

33. Field, Margaret J., *Search for Security,* (London, 1960) p. 107.

34. G. E. Hurd, "Education," in *A Study of Contemporary Ghana: Some Aspects of Social Structure* ed. Birmingham et al., II, 226.

35. S. Otoo, "The Actual Need for Christian Healing Ministry," *The Ghana Bulletin of Theology,* 3, 2 (June, 1967), 21.

List of Works Cited

"African Christian Needs New Awakening." Sunday *Mirror* (Jan. 23, 1966), p. 4.

Acquah, Ione. *Accra Survey.* London, 1958.

Amoah, Frank E. K. *Accra: A Study of the Development of a West African City.* Unpublished thesis, Institute of African Studies, University of Ghana, Legon, 1964.

Andersson, Efraim. *Churches at the Grass Roots: A Study in Congo-Brazzaville. New York, 1962.*

———. *Messianic Popular Movements in the Lower Congo.* Uppsala, 1958.

Anquandah, J. R. "Editorial." *The Torch,* I, 3 (June 1968), 1—2.

———. "Panorama." *The Torch,* I, 4 (October 1968), 7—9.

Anquandah, James. "Brother Yeboa-Korie and the Eden Revival Church." *The Edenian,* I, 1 (January—February 1968), 2—4.

Ayandele, E. A. *The Missionary Impact on Modern Nigeria.* London, 1966.

Baeta, Christian G. "Aspects of Religion." In *A Study of Contemporary Ghana: Some Aspects of Social Structure,* ed. Walter Birmingham et al., II, 240—50. London, 1967.

———. *Prophetism in Ghana.* London, 1962.

Barrett, David B. "A. D. 2000: 350 Million Christians in Africa." *International Review of Missions,* 59 (1970), 39—53.

———. *Schism and Renewal in Africa.* London, 1968.

Bartels, F. L. *The Roots of Ghana Methodism.* Cambridge, England, 1965.

Beckmann, David M. "Trance: From Africa to Pentecostalism." *CTM,* XLV, 1 (January 1974), 11—26.

Bennett, George. "Christianity and African Nationalism." *Mawazo,* I, 3 (June 1968), 65.

Birmingham, Walter, I. Neustadt, and E. N. Omaboe. *A Study of Contemporary Ghana: The Economy of Ghana.* London, 1967.

Bourguignon, Erika. "World Distribution and Patterns of Possession States." In *Trance and Possession States,* ed. Raymond Prince, pp. 3 – 34. Montreal, 1968.

Bracey, John H., Jr., August Meier, and Elliot Rudwick, eds. *American Slavery: The Question of Resistance.* Belmont, Calif., 1971.

1960 Census Special Report A: Statistics of Large Towns. Ghana Census, 1960.

Central Bureau of Statistics. *Quarterly Digest of Statistics,* XV and XVIII. Ghana, 1966 and 1968.

"Christian Council Speaks," *Mirror* (Feb. 6, 1966), p. 14.

Clark, Robert R. "An Appeal to Our Universities on Behalf of the Heathen and Mohammedan World." *The Church Missionary Intelligencer,* VI (London, 1871), 46 – 47.

Cnattingius, Hans Jacob. *Bishops and Societies.* London, 1952.

Cone, James H. *A Black Theology of Liberation.* Philadelphia and New York, 1970.

Consultation on the Healing Ministry of the Church. "Findings and Questions." *The Ghana Bulletin of Theology,* 3, 2 – 3 (December 1967), 28.

Crowder, Michael. *West Africa Under Colonial Rule.* London, 1968.

Curtin, Philip. *The Image of Africa.* Madison, Wis., 1964.

Debrunner, Hans W. *A History of Christianity in Ghana.* Accra, 1968.

——. *Witchcraft in Ghana.* Accra, 1961.

Dickson, Kwamina B. *A Historical Geography of Ghana.* Cambridge, England, 1964.

Dretke, James P. *A Study of Moslems in Accra.* Unpublished thesis, Institute of African Studies, University of Ghana, Legon, 1965.

Eden Church Secretariat. *Eden Revival Church of Ghana Handbook.* Accra, 1971.

"Exit King '67." *The Edenian,* I, 1 (January-February 1968), 2.

"Exploiters in the Name of the Church." *Evening News,* April 10, 1965.

Fiawoo, D. K. "From Cult to Church: A Study of Some Aspects of Religious Change in Ghana." *Ghana Journal of Sociology,* IV, 2 (October 1968), 72—87.

Field, Margaret J. *Religion and Medicine of the Ga People.* London, 1937.

——. *Search for Security.* London, 1960.

Fitch, Bob, and Mary Oppenheimer. *Ghana: End of an Illusion.* New York and London, 1966.

Frazier, E. Franklin. *The Negro Church in America.* New York, 1964.

Fyfe, Christopher. *A History of Sierra Leone.* London, 1962.

Gil, B., A. F. Aryee, and D. K. Ghansah. *1960 Population Census of Ghana: Special Report "E," Tribes in Ghana.* Accra, 1964.

The Gold Coast 1931. Appendices Containing Comparative Returns and General Statistics of the 1931 Census. Accra, 1932.

The Gold Coast: Census of Population 1948 Report and Tables. London, 1950.

Goody, Jack. "Anomie in Ashante?" *Africa,* XXVII (London, 1957), 356—63.

Groves, C. P. *The Planting of Christianity in Africa.* 4 vols. London, 1958.

Haliburton, Gordon M. *The Prophet Harris.* New York, 1973. 1965.

Herskovits, Melville J. *The New World Negro.* Bloomington, Ind., 1966.

Hinson, E. Glenn. "A Brief History of Glossolalia," In *Glossolalia,* by Frank Stagg, E. Glenn Hinson, and Wayne E. Oates, pp. 47—56. Nashville and New York, 1967.

Hollenweger, Walter J. *Handbuch der Pfingstbewegung.* Geneva, 1966—67.

——. *The Pentecostals.* Minneapolis, 1972.

Hurd, G. E. "Education." In *A Study of Contemporary Ghana: Some Aspects of Social Structure,* II, ed. Walter Birmingham et al., 217—39. London, 1967.

Jackson, Bruce, ed. *The Negro and His Folklore in Nineteenth Century Periodicals.* Austin and London, 1967.

Jehu-Appiah, Moses. Letter to the author, June 21, 1970.

Kessler, J. B. A. "Let's Spend Mission Dollars More Wisely." *World Vision,* 13, 5 (May 1969), 4.

Knox, R. A. *Enthusiasm.* Oxford, 1950.

Lanternari, Vittorio. *The Religions of the Oppressed,* trans. Lisa Sergio. New York, 1963.

Marshall, M. J. *Christianity and Nationalism in Ghana.* Unpublished thesis, Institute of African Studies, University of Ghana, Legon, 1965.

Martin, Marie-Louise. *Kirche ohne Weisse.* Basel, 1971.

May, L. Carlyle. "A Survey of Glossolalia and Related Phenomena in Non-Christian Religions." *American Anthropologist,* XLVIII (1956), 75−93.

The Methodist Church. *Annual Reports 1900, 1912, 1921, 1941, 1951, 1961.*
———. *Conference Schedules 1961−68.*
The Methodist Church. *Minutes of the Gold Coast District Synod and Missionary Meeting 1930.*

Mitchell, Robert. "The Aladura in Ibadan." Paper presented to the Social Science Seminar, University College, Ibadan, March 1962. 12 pp.

Ntiforo, S. R., and P. Rutishauser. "Prayer Groups and Sects." Report presented to 1966 Synod of the Presbyterian Church of Ghana. Accra, 1966.

The Office of the Government Statistician. *Digest of Statistics,* V, 1−2. Gold Coast, 1956.

Opoku, K. A. "A History of Independent Churches in Ghana, 1862−1969." Unpublished paper.

———. "The Universal Prayer Group−'Mpaebo Kuw' (Adoagyiri, Nsawam)−The Call of the Prophet." *Institute of African Studies Research Review,* V, 1 (Michaelmas Term 1968), 101−108.

Otoo, S. "The Actual Need for Christian Healing Ministry." *The Ghana Bulletin of Theology,* 3, 2 (June 1967), 20−23.

Parrinder, Geoffrey. *Religion in an African City*. London, 1953.

Parsons, Robert T. *The Churches and Ghana Society 1918–1955*. Leiden, 1963.

Peel, J. D. Y. *Aladura: A Religious Movement Among the Yoruba*. London, 1968.

Platt, W. J. *An African Prophet*. London, 1934.

Presbyterian Church of Ghana. *Reports 1960–68*.

Rattray, R. Sutherland. *Religion and Art in Ashanti*. London, 1927.

Shepperson, George, and Thomas Price. *Independent African*. Edinburgh, 1968.

Statistical Handbook of the Republic of Ghana 1967. Central Bureau of Statistics, Accra.

Sundkler, Bengt G. M. *Bantu Prophets in South Africa*. London, 1961.

Taylor, John V. "Christianity in Africa." *Africa: A Handbook to the Continent,* ed. Colin Legum. London, 1961.

——. *The Primal Vision*. London, 1963.

——, and Dorothea Lehmann. *Christians of the Copperbelt*. Liverpool and London, 1961.

Tetteh, P. A. "Marriage, Family and Household." *A Study of Contemporary Ghana: Some Aspects of Social Structure,* ed. Birmingham et al., 201–16. London, 1967.

"The Truth About You and Your Star." *The Torch*. I, 3 (June, 1968), 4.

Tinney, James S. "Black Origins of the Pentecostal Movement." *Christianity Today,* XVI, 1 (Oct. 8, 1971), 4–6.

Turner, H. W. *African Independent Church: The Life and Faith of the Church of the Lord (Aladura),* II. London, 1967.

——. "The Church of the Lord: The Expansion of a Nigerian Independent Church in Sierra Leone and Ghana." *Journal of African History,* III, 1 (1962), 91–110.

——. "The Place of Independent Religious Movements in the Modernization of Africa." 20 pp.

Ward, Barbara E. "Some Observations on Religious Cults in Ashanti." *Africa,* XXVI (London, 1956), 47–60.

Warren, Max. *Social History and Christian Mission*. London, 1967.

143

Weaver, Edwin and Irene. *The Uyo Story*. Elkhart, Ind., 1970.

Webster, James Bertin. *The African Church Among the Yoruba 1888 – 1922*. London, 1964.

Welbourne, F. B. *East African Christian*. Ibadan, 1965.

——. *East.African Rebels*. London, 1961.

——, and B. A. Ogot. *A Place to Feel at Home*. London, 1966.

Wesley, John. *Journal,* ed. Nehemiah Curnock. London, 1938.

Wiedner, Donald L. *A History of Africa South of the Sahara*. New York, 1962.

Wishlade, R. L. *Sectarianism in Southern Nyasaland*. London, 1965.

World Christian Handbook. Nashville and New York, 1967.

Yeboa-Korie, Charles. "Christian Spiritual Development." *The Edenian,* I, 2 (February-March 1968), 1; *The Torch,* I, 3 (June 1968), 3, and I, 4 (October 1968), 3.